Helion & Company Limited
Unit 8 Amherst Business Centre
Budbrooke Road
Warwick
CV34 5WE
England
Tel. 01926 499 619
Email: info@helion.co.uk
Website: www.helion.co.uk
Twitter: @helionbooks
Visit our blog http://blog.helion.co.uk/

Text © Edward Crowther 2023
Photographs © as individually credited
Colour artwork © Giorgio Albertini, David
    Bocquelet, and Anderson Subtil 2023
Maps © Paul Hewitt and Tiago Alexandre
    Batista 2023

Designed and typeset by Farr out
    Publications, Wokingham, Berkshire
Cover design Paul Hewitt, Battlefield Design
    (www.battlefield-design.co.uk)

ISBN 978-1-804512-17-3

British Library Cataloguing-in-Publication
    Data
A catalogue record for this book is available
    from the British Library

We always welcome receiving book
proposals from prospective authors.

CONTENTS

MAP OF EUROPE SINCE 1992

Note: In order to simplify the use of this book, all names, locations and geographic designations are as provided in *The Times World Atlas*, or other traditionally accepted major sources of reference, as of the time of described events.

ABBREVIATIONS

ATO	Anti-Terrorist Operation	**MGB**	Lugansk People's Republic State Security Ministry
CBRN	Chemical, Biological, Radiological, and Nuclear (formerly referred to as NBC/Nuclear, Biological, Chemical)	**MLRS**	Multiple Launch Rocket System
		NATO	North Atlantic Treaty Organization
DPR	Donetsk People's Republic	**SBU**	Ukrainian State Security Services
LPR	Luhansk People's Republic	**UAV**	Unmanned/Uncrewed Aerial Vehicle
MANPADS	Man-Portable Air Defence Systems		

INTRODUCTION AND ACKNOWLEDGEMENTS

This book is about the armed formations of the Luhansk People's Republic (LPR), a de facto political entity in eastern Ukraine, covering a period in time from its creation in 2014 to September 2022, when the LPR was annexed by the Russian Federation.

The armed formations of the LPR were assembled from a very diverse array of armed anti-government groups that sprang up in Luhansk oblast in 2014.[1] This book aims to increase understanding of this process of force generation, and the role that the LPR's armed formations played as a key proxy force used by the Kremlin in eastern Ukraine.

This book seeks to bring the armed formations of the LPR during this period into greater focus, explaining the history of their creation, motivational ideology, structure, capabilities and equipment. Though of course dwarfed by the military resources fielded by the Russian Federation, in the years between 2014 and 2022 the armed formations of the DPR (Donetsk People's Republic) and LPR together numbered some 40,000 people. Despite being a sizeable proxy force for the Russian Federation, in much reporting on the conflict they were often passed over in a single line as 'separatist' or 'pro-Russian' forces.

The relationship of the LPR with its patron state, the Russian Federation, will also be explored. Here, the terminology of the study of proxy warfare will be employed, and the complex and changing nature of the relationship between the 'benefactor' (Russia) and the 'proxy' (the LPR) will be examined.[2]

For much of its existence, the LPR was riven with internal rivalries as competing power blocs fought each other. This created problems for the Kremlin as it struggled to keep its proxy creation under control. This is not to absolve the Kremlin of responsibility in

sparking and then fanning the flames of conflict in Donbas, thereby turning hitherto mostly peaceful political differences into an armed conflict that had – by the end of 2021 – already claimed around 14,000 lives. After Russia's full-scale invasion of early 2022, the death toll has jumped by thousands and at the time of writing continues to climb.

Russia acted from 2014 to early 2022 as the sole 'security guarantor' for the two People's Republics in eastern Ukraine. The Kremlin sought to lower international accountability for the ensuing violence in Donbas by building in degrees of 'plausible deniability' and political separation from the Russian state. This separation was not without cost though, as there were serious problems of command and control that manifested in the often unruly, chaotic and violent nature of the LPR's armed formations in the early days of the conflict.[3]

Residents wave to LPR militants sitting atop a BTR-80 armoured personnel carrier during a parade in the city of Luhansk on 14 September 2014. The non-standardised nature of the early armed formations of the LPR in 2014 is well demonstrated here, with a wide range of camouflage uniforms alongside civilian dress. Light weapons on display include the standard AK-74 5.45mm assault rifle, RPK variants and a PK 7.62mm general purpose machinegun. (Associated Press/Alamy Stock Photo)

The relatively static or 'frozen' nature of the conflict in eastern Ukraine between 2015 and 2022 was altered, first by the official recognition of the DPR and LPR as independent states by the Russian Federation on 21 February 2022, and then by the start of the massive Russian 'special military operation' into Ukraine that began on 24 February 2022.

Marking a sudden and seismic shift in policy, Putin announced a 'special military operation' in Ukraine commencing on 24 February 2022. One of the stated goals for this 'special military operation' was to come to the aid of the Donetsk and Luhansk People's Republics, and Putin referred to the treaties of 'friendship and mutual assistance' that had been ratified only two days earlier.[4]

The outcome of this 'special military operation' was, at the time of writing, still to be determined. Supported by massive military forces which streamed across the border from the Russian Federation, the armed formations of the LPR pushed to the boundaries of pre-conflict Luhansk oblast, and for a brief time appeared to have reached their stated pre-February 2022 goals, namely control over all of Luhansk oblast. Many of the cities that stood in their path: Severodonetsk, Lysychansk, Rubizhne, Popasna and more besides, were massively damaged in the fighting. Thousands of people had been killed and injured.

This book aims to be historical rather than predictive in its formulation, and will outline the turbulent creation and often chaotic nature of the armed formations of the LPR from 2014 to February 2022 when these formations joined Putin's 'special military operation.' After this, the period until the formal annexation of the LPR and DPR into the Russian Federation in September 2022 will also be covered.

Scope of Focus

By focusing on the LPR's armed formations, the role of Russian Federation regular units will be discussed where relevant, but for a necessary limitation of scope this book will not examine these units in great detail. Similarly, the much-publicised role of the Russian Private Military Company (PMC) Wagner Group, in particular at Debaltseve in 2015 and at Bakhmut after February 2022, is touched upon though in a similar fashion this PMC and its use by Russia in Donbas is not the book's primary focus.

Methodology

This book was written entirely from open-source information, utilising sources in the Ukrainian, Russian and English languages. It aims to collect and synthesise these various information sources and provide a concise and readable account of the LPR's armed formations, in particular for the reader who may be less familiar with some of the disparate information sources available on the conflict in eastern Ukraine.

As this book is about the LPR's armed formations, a primary source of information was LPR reports or media statements, or articles about the LPR in 'sympathetic' media outlets. However, as information warfare of all kinds was a major feature of the conflict in eastern Ukraine from 2014 to 2022, such reports obviously have to read with this in mind.

A second major source of information was Ukrainian or Western open-source investigation and reporting into the LPR's capabilities. Ukrainian open-source investigation was usually incredibly detailed, and often written with the benefit of a deep understanding of the terrain and actors involved.

However, for various understandable reasons, which will be discussed in more depth below, Ukrainian sources tended to place a much greater emphasis on the role of the Russian Federation in the LPR's armed formations, often denying any form of 'agency' on the part of the LPR at all.

The book therefore attempts to synthesise various sources of information about the LPR's armed formations and present them in what it hopes will be a balanced way.

Terms/naming conventions/transliteration

Any writing about the LPR and the Ukraine conflict has to take a position on naming and terminology.

Definition of areas

This is a book primarily about the armed formations of the LPR, which was for the period of focus of the book the de facto entity in control of a significant part of Luhansk oblast in eastern Ukraine. Those areas in eastern Ukraine not under the control of the Ukrainian state were called different things, usually depending on the political position of the speaker.

For those who refused to use the term 'Luhansk People's Republic,' there were a number of other names available. Some authors and international organisations favoured 'Non-Government-Controlled Areas' (NGCA) or 'Certain Areas of Luhansk Oblast' (CALO), in addition the term 'Occupied Regions of Donetsk and Luhansk Oblasts' (ORDiLO) was also sometimes used.[5]

The situation in Ukraine, after the stabilisation of the contact line in 2015 until February 2022. Ukraine's two eastern oblasts of Donetsk and Luhansk are indicated (other oblasts in Ukraine are not shown for clarity). The red line is the contact line, to the east of which were the two non-government-controlled areas occupied by the DPR and LPR. The Crimean peninsula, occupied from 2014 onwards by the Russian Federation, is similarly indicated. (Tiago Alexandre Batista)

After mid-2015, when the initially highly fluid territorial control picture in Donbas solidified into a static front line which barely changed until February 2022, around 8,700 square kilometres of Luhansk oblast were estimated to be under the control of the LPR.[6] This area amounted to only 33 percent of the oblast's pre-conflict area, though this area contained many of the oblast's key cities such as the capital Luhansk, and major industrial cities such as Alchevsk and Kadiivka.

The LPR existed from 2014 to 2022 as a de facto entity of uncertain status in the territorial area of eastern Ukraine, lacking formal international recognition even from their patron state, the Russian Federation. The best definition for the LPR during this time is probably that of an 'unrecognised state', following the work of the academic Nina Caspersen on such entities. She suggests that an unrecognised state must meet the following criteria:

1) The entity has achieved de facto independence.
2) Its leadership is seeking to build further state institutions and demonstrate its own legitimacy.
3) The entity has sought, but not achieved, international recognition.
4) It has existed for at least 2 years.[7]

However, de facto independence did not equate to automatic demands for statehood, and as one Ukrainian academic noted in 2018, '…there is no complete picture of whether today's Luhansk and Donetsk 'republics' are states or, if not, what their administrative and territorial status really is … So, in the Donetsk 'republic's' schools, the region is studied as part of courses concerning geographical matters, and in the curriculums and textbooks of these courses the Donbas is merely called an "area" (край).'[8]

Definition of organisations

After declaring its independence in 2014, the LPR quickly launched into building state-like institutions, usually mimicking those of its benefactor state, Russia. In addition to the armed formations which are the primary focus of this book, these included replicating all the functions of government, including line ministries and administrative organisations.

It was understandably common in pro-Ukrainian circles to refer to such institutions in inverted commas, in order to reject their legitimacy, or similarly to prefix the titles of ministers or other functionaries of the LPR with words such as 'so-called' or 'self-proclaimed' for a similar reason. Under Ukrainian law, the LPR and its armed formations were quickly classified as terrorist organisations.

For the purposes of clarity, this book will refer to LPR armed formations, ministries, organisations, and the people in charge of them as they would have referred to themselves. This is to aid comprehension and clarity, and does not imply acceptance or confer legitimacy.

Place names

In 2015, Ukraine enacted a series of laws on decommunisation, which aimed to remove references to the country's Soviet past. As a result, thousands of streets, villages, towns and cities were renamed, and Communist-era statues and memorials removed. As a side note, many commonly used online mapping websites and softwares had by 2022 yet to change many places to the new official names.

For the DPR and LPR, a rejection of this attempt to erase the Soviet past became one of the most obvious visual differences between Ukraine and the two non-government-controlled areas in Donbas. As statues of Lenin were taken down across the rest of Ukraine, they remained standing in the DPR and LPR-controlled cities of Donetsk, Luhansk, Ilovaisk, Alchevsk, and many others.

As this book refers to places within the international-recognised territory of Ukraine, and for consistency, it will utilise those place names officially designated by the Ukrainian state, though in places may also sometimes append the former place name in addition to aid comprehension.

The most striking example from Luhansk oblast may be the example of the coal mining town of Kadiivka, renamed Stakhanov in 1978 after the famous Soviet coal miner Aleksei Stakhanov. Ukraine's 2015 decommunisation laws changed the name of the city back to Kadiivka, but this name change had little traction in the LPR-controlled city at the time.

Similarly, the anglicised variants of Ukrainian place names will be utilised, such as 'Donbas' rather than 'Donbass.'[9] Where someone else is being quoted, the spelling in the original text will be retained.

Linguistic note

The Luhansk People's Republic (LPR) is sometimes found referred to in some English language material as LNR, this stems from a direct transliteration of the LPR's acronym in Russian: *Luhanskaya Narodnaya Respublika*.

Elsewhere, there may be small differences in the spelling of certain people's names, owing to differing transliterations from Ukrainian or Russian. The book attempts to maintain consistency in its own spellings throughout, but retains the spellings of people's names in quotations as per the original.

Acknowledgements

Many people contributed to the completion of this book. Special thanks go to Tiago Alexandre Batista for the maps, and to Tom, Andy and Duncan at Helion for the patient understanding and constant support.

1
ORIGINS OF THE CONFLICT IN EASTERN UKRAINE

In order to understand the LPR's armed formations and the creation of the LPR itself, it is necessary to situate them within the origins of the conflict in eastern Ukraine in 2014, and its place within rising geostrategic conflict between Russia and the West that had been gathering pace since 2007.

The causes of the conflict in eastern Ukraine had their origins in both geostrategic conflict between Russia and the West, and growing internal divisions within Ukraine. As the Ukrainian scholar Serhy Yekelchyk noted: 'The fighting in … Donetsk and Luhansk provinces combines features of a covert foreign invasion with those of a civil conflict. Accordingly, it has both external and internal causes, even if these happen to be closely connected.'[1]

Russian ressentiment and NATO expansion

After the breakup of the Soviet Union, Russia found itself bordered by newly-independent former Soviet republics, as well as former Warsaw Pact states in eastern Europe. The sharp economic decline caused by the breakup of the Soviet Union also left Russia unable to challenge what it saw as the unwelcome hegemony of the United States and its allies over global affairs, and in particular the West's growing influence over what Russia viewed as its traditional spheres of influence. 'The disparity between limited resources and lingering pretensions was the source of much confusion and frustration, the foundation for a great-power nostalgia.'[2]

This lingering great power nostalgia, implicit in the Russian word *derzhava* (great power), had fateful implications. Over the course of the 1990s and 2000s, NATO and the European Union eagerly welcomed to their ranks newly-democratic, former Warsaw Pact countries like Poland, Hungary and Romania, as well as former Soviet Republics like Estonia, Latvia, and Lithuania. 'Russia's weakness after 1991 freed the West … to pursue its own strategic designs, foremost among them the expansion of NATO. In the face of Western dominance, Russia was compelled to accept these moves as *faits accomplis*.'[3]

The relationship between Russia and the West was further soured by the NATO campaign in Yugoslavia in the late 1990s, and the 2003 invasion of Iraq. In the minds of Russian policymakers, these campaigns demonstrated that the West was willing to act unilaterally when it suited Western – and in particular American – interests. The invasion of Iraq, which Russia openly objected to and opposed, came only a few years after Russia had provided what it saw as enthusiastic support for the US-led Global War on Terror after 2001.

In May 2008, at the NATO summit in Bucharest, NATO took the fateful decision of offering possible future membership to both Georgia and Ukraine. Both were offered a promise that their applications for Membership Action Plans would be reviewed in December that same year.[4] There was in fact little appetite among some key NATO members to include Ukraine or Georgia, and as one critic of the decision pointed out, '…some Western countries in NATO and the European Union had, over many years, unrealistically raised Ukraine's expectation of joining these bodies, leaving Ukraine without formal allies but badly exposed to Russian aggression.'[5]

At the end of the Bucharest Summit, Vladimir Putin gave a speech which was a veiled warning against further NATO expansion eastwards. In addition, increasing references were being made in Russia to the supposed promises given by Western politicians at the end of the Cold War that NATO would not extend its membership eastwards.

After the summit, the diplomatic relationship between Russia and Georgia deteriorated rapidly, culminating in the brief, violent war between Russia and Georgia in August 2008. As Wood notes, '…the Georgia operation was more immediately intended to call the West's bluff on further NATO enlargement … [While] the issue of Ukraine – strategically far more significant to both Russia and the West – lurked in the background, as an obvious future flashpoint.'[6]

Dynamics within Ukraine

In order to more fully comprehend the LPR as a political entity, and its armed formations, it is necessary to situate the LPR within a brief discussion of the history and politics of modern Ukraine – a full exploration of which would vastly exceed the scope of this book.

There has been a tendency, in particular in journalistic shorthand, to describe Ukraine as being divided into western Ukraine, seen as more pro-Western, and eastern Ukraine which is seen as more pro-Russian. Some commentators on Ukraine went as far as to equate 'Russian-speaking' as being tantamount to 'pro-Russian' in political leanings. The truth was, however, more complex, and in Ukraine '… there was no single identity cleavage – the question was never so simple as Russian or Ukrainian.'[7]

Broadly summarised, the differences in language and culture within Ukraine stemmed from historical periods and processes which affected the various regions in divergent ways. Parts of western Ukraine were part of the Austro-Hungarian Empire well into the twentieth century, whereas eastern Ukraine developed under Russian and then Soviet rule.

In eastern Ukraine, and the Donbas in particular, heavy industrialisation and cultural 'Russification' were promoted by first the Russian Empire and the Soviets that followed. In western Ukraine, the Austro-Hungarian Empire discouraged industrialisation, while also allowing the teaching of the Ukrainian language. This meant that Ukrainian culture continued to flourish in western Ukraine.

Parts of what are now western Ukraine were finally brought under Soviet rule at the end of the Polish-Soviet War in 1921 and after the partition of Poland in the Second World War, but consequently spent less time under Soviet rule until the final collapse of the Soviet Union in 1991.

Writing about Ukraine, one author noted that: 'Empires, with their attendant histories of hierarchy, conquest and exploitation, involving humiliation for some and glory for others, deposit their influence on later generations in complex and ever-evolving ways.'[8] As a result, '…the divergent experiences of western Ukrainians and their kin in the south and east have left their mark … in the form of differences on matters ranging from identity and internal politics to foreign policy. These differences would reemerge in 2013 – 2014 and segue into a clash between Russia and the West over Ukraine's future.'[9]

Politically, and with similar broad summarisation, following independence in 1991 Ukraine was ruled by a series of presidents who tried to tread different paths between the West and Russia. In 2014, the president was Viktor Yanukovych, against whom the Euro Maidan protests of 2013–14 erupted in Kyiv. These protests, and the outcome of them, will be discussed in more detail below.

Donbas region

The Donbas – its name a portmanteau of the words Donets River Basin – was in the early nineteenth century a remote and underdeveloped part of the Russian Empire, dominated by the open and sparsely populated steppe. There were only small and scattered settlements across the steppe, notably the Cossack *stanytsias*, a word that survives today for example in the place name of Stanytsia Luhanska, a town on the Siverskyi Donets River in Luhansk oblast, heavily fought over in 2014 and again in 2022.

The industrialisation of the Donbas region began in the period of the Russian Empire, when concessions were opened to foreign companies and experts in order to import advanced manufacturing technologies and begin heavy industrial enterprises in certain regions of the empire. This was spurred on in part by Russia's humiliating defeat in the Crimean War, in which the allied and technologically superior Ottoman, British and French forces had been able to move more rapidly by sea than had Russian forces using their road network, spurring a Russian desire for an improved railway system.

The Donbas was among the regions earmarked for this rapid industrial development. Realising they needed foreign expertise and investment to fully develop the region, the Imperial Russian government invited entrepreneurs from abroad. The city of Luhansk was founded in 1795 by a Scottish engineer, Charles Gascoigne, who opened a metal factory there, also bringing to the Russian government advanced weapons designs and manufacturing techniques, in particular for carronades. His statue still stands in Luhansk outside the city museum.

In a similar fashion, a Welsh engineer called John Hughes founded the city that would later become Donetsk in 1869, whereas Belgian industrial concerns developed what is now the Ukrainian city of Kostiantynivka in Donetsk oblast. French and German companies were also present across the region. In Luhansk, a major railway locomotive factory, the Russische Maschinenbaugesellschaft Hartmann, was built by the German engineer Gustav Hartmann in 1869, and continued producing railway equipment until it finally closed (owing to the conflict) in 2015.

Plentiful coal deposits found in the Donbas were linked by railway line to rich iron ore deposits found at Kriviy Rih in what is now central Ukraine, and the resulting boom in metallurgical production attracted workers from across the Russian Empire and abroad, creating a multi-ethnic society with Russian as the standard *lingua franca*. The legacy of this industrial past was left in the names of towns across Luhansk, such as Antratsyt (anthracite) and Metalist. Crucially, the industrial cities and societies that attracted Russian-speaking workers from across the Russian Empire were culturally distinct from the Ukrainian agrarian society around them.

By 1917 the Donbas was one of the key industrial regions in the Soviet Union when all foreign enterprises were nationalised by the Soviets after the October Revolution. Industrial workers, such as those of the Donbas and other heavy industrial regions like Magnitogorsk, were designated as priority workers by the Soviet regime. They thus received favourable treatment in Soviet society in the form of better housing as well as access to holidays and healthcare. Thus the Donbas '…the coal-rich area in Eastern Ukraine and part of Russia's Rostov region, became the cradle of a quintessential Soviet identity.'[10]

Nowhere was this more aptly displayed than in the town of Kadiivka in Luhansk oblast. At the Tsentralnaya-Irmino coal mine, in September 1935, a coal miner called Alexei Stakhanov allegedly mined 227 tonnes of coal in a single shift, breaking his individual quota many times over. Though there is now some historical debate about the extent to which it was in fact a team effort, it was widely reported at the time.

Seizing upon this propaganda victory, the Soviet Union showered him with rewards including the Hero of Soviet Labour, and in the West he appeared on the cover of *Time* magazine. The word 'Stakhanovite' even entered the English language, denoting an exceptionally hard worker. After his death in 1977, the town of Kadiivka '…was renamed in his honour, the only Soviet city to bear the name of a humble worker.'[11]

Despite their strong affiliation with the Soviet Union, the Donbas miners staged a series of strikes in 1991, during which they demanded state sovereignty for Ukraine. This was largely due to the creaking Soviet economy, and worsening conditions for miners and other industrial workers.

After the Soviet Union collapsed and Ukraine won its independence, the Donbas, which had been heavily reliant on 'all-

A medal 'For the Restoration of the Donbass Coal Mines' («За восстановление угольных шахт Донбасса»), awarded from 1947 onwards to those who helped restore the coalmines of the Donbas after the destruction wrought during the Second World War. Such medals helped cement the sense of pride many inhabitants of Donbas felt as part of the Soviet system. (Author's collection)

Union' trade, found itself in steep economic decline as the traditional industries closed down or were seized by oligarchs at knock-down prices. The 1990s in Donbas thus '…saw working men and women undergo a humiliating transformation from the Soviet Union's most privileged class to one living among a cancer of crime, poverty, gambling and oligarchy.'[12]

Furthermore, as Ukrainian national identity underwent a nascent revival, '…a new national ideology began to dominate in Ukraine, wherein the 'proletarian' Donbas, Russian-speaking and rooted in Soviet culture, could have only a marginal position.'[13] The Ukrainian government began replacing the old Soviet symbols and heroes – such as the aforementioned Stakhanov – with a new set of national symbols. This was unpopular among many in the Donbas, where the symbols of the Soviet past formed a large part of their identity.

During this period of increasing mutual misunderstanding, '…the Donbas continued to be alienated by stories of aggressive Ukrainian 'fascists' and their attempts to humiliate the region's inhabitants of by replacing their heroes with strangers, and imposing a 'wrong' version of history and 'rural' Ukrainian language and culture.'[14] This growing mistrust between Ukrainians later left the door open for foreign influence. 'Intra-Ukrainian regional stereotyping also increased Ukraine's vulnerability to Russian predation.'[15]

Euro Maidan

By 2013, the growing geopolitical rivalry between Russia and the West came to a head in Ukraine. The then president was Viktor

Yanukovych, a native of Donetsk oblast who in earlier life had worked in the coal mining industry. The European Union was offering Ukraine an Association Agreement, and Russia – who had backed Yanukovych's political campaign – was placing pressure on Ukraine to not sign, and was instead offering an alternative trade deal.

At the last minute, Yanukovych backed out of the deal with the EU. This sparked a protest on the Maidan, the large square at the centre of Kyiv. Organised by social media, the initially small protest soon swelled into a huge gathering of protestors.[16] Though initially about the government's failure to sign the agreement with the EU, the protest quickly widened into a larger one in which people were protesting against the country's future path. Many protestors wanted closer links with Europe and the wider West, and were decrying the influence of oligarchs and corruption over Ukrainian society.

For its part, the Kremlin looked on with horror as the Maidan protest grew in size. They saw it as yet another example of the 'Colour Revolutions' which had swept across the former Soviet space after the collapse of the Soviet Union, in which popular protests had ousted or attempted to oust incumbent (usually pro-Russian) governments. To the Kremlin, it was not possible that these protests could be at all spontaneous or homegrown, the former men from the security agencies thought that behind all of the protestors there must be the influence of the West and its agents, a form of hybrid warfare being waged against Russia.

Increasingly desperate and under pressure from both the protestors on Maidan and the Kremlin on the telephone, Yanukovych attempted to use force to disperse the protestors. As well as deploying the 'Berkut' riot police, thousands of men were bussed in from the surrounding regions and paid to pose as 'anti-Maidan' protestors, violently attacking the protestors on the Maidan. These men were informally referred to as *titushki* and many were brought from Donbas where Yanukovych had a lot of political support.[17] Later, remnants of both the 'Berkut' riot police and *titushki* bussed in from Donbas would form the nucleus of some of the early armed formations of the DPR and LPR.

Over a hundred people were killed on the Maidan, and many more injured. In February 2014, with his support crumbling, Yanukovych fled Ukraine for Russia and an interim government was put in place. Both the Kremlin, as well as many inhabitants of eastern Ukraine, viewed Yanukovych as the legitimate elected leader of Ukraine. Many in Donbas therefore perceived the Maidan as the violent overthrow of a legitimate government.

As a result, there followed a wave of anti-Maidan protests across southern and eastern Ukraine, in which there were often violent clashes with pro-Maidan groups. The ensuring violence during these clashes gave much fuel to Russian psychological warfare. This set the scene for the coming confrontation in the Donbas, where anti-government sentiment was now rife.

Seizure of Crimea

After the fall of the Yanukovych government in Ukraine in the wake of the Maidan protests, the Kremlin moved swiftly and decisively to seize the Crimean peninsula. Crimea was of vital strategic importance to Russia in the eyes of the Kremlin, in particular owing to the presence of the Sevastopol naval base which Russia had been leasing from Ukraine since the collapse of the Soviet Union. In addition, the population of Crimea were highly pro-Russian, and in polling since independence had consistently expressed a desire for closer ties with Russia.

After the events at Maidan, the new interim Ukrainian government was disorganised and focused on internal problems. Almost no attention was paid to distant Crimea, where, on '…28 February … up to fourteen Ilyushin-76 aircraft delivered an estimated 1,400 Spetsnaz to the Gvardeiskoye airfield near Simferopol … The element of surprise … coupled with their unexpected sophistication, all contributed to the shock and awe that allowed Russia to swifty annex the peninsula without any bloodshed.'[18] These regular Russian Federation forces came to be referred to as 'Little Green Men' in the Western media, but more commonly referred to in Russian media as 'Polite People,' owing to the polite but firm way they refused to answer any questions.

By early March 2014, Russian forces had taken complete control over the Crimean peninsula, and had cut if off from the rest of Ukraine. They were aided by various proxy forces comprising '… Afghan veterans, boxers, *Nochnye Volki* (Night Wolves) bikers, members of territorial army (DOSAAF) clubs and private security guards. They collected intelligence, identified potential saboteurs, stood guard at pro-Russia rallies, "neutralised" opponents and participated in overtaking military objects and administrative buildings disguised as local residents.'[19] It was this mixing of regular and irregular forces that had important ramifications for the way the Ukrainian government and the wider world viewed the conflict that erupted shortly afterwards in Donbas.

Two men on a motorbike flying a Communist flag and that of the Luhansk chapter of the 'Night Wolves' motorcycle gang, Luhansk city 14 September 2014. One man carries an AK-74 slung over his shoulder. The 'Night Wolves' had also played a role in the earlier seizure of Crimea in March. (Associated Press/Alamy Stock Photo)

Overseen by these units of Russian special and irregular forces, a referendum on Crimea's status was held across the peninsula on 16 March 2014. The referendum was widely condemned as illegal by the Ukrainian government and in the West. The result of this heavily stage-managed referendum was overwhelmingly in favour of joining the Russian Federation, and on 17 March 2014 Russia formally annexed Crimea into its territory, ignoring the loud international condemnation that accompanied the move.

The shocking events in Crimea had a fateful impact on the Donbas in eastern Ukraine. For pro-Russian elements in the Donbas

'…in Crimea, as well as in Eastern Ukraine … Russia's sudden decisiveness gave them permission to act. Crimeans and Eastern Ukrainians who had supported Russia passively until then suddenly had enormous additional incentives to do so actively.'[20]

Many of those who did then 'act' undoubtedly hoped for a similarly swift and bloodless campaign. As one study of pro-Russian paramilitary motivation in Donbas noted: 'The expectation of 'the Crimean scenario' … that would secure the position of pro-Russian fighters was common for all groups.'[21]

2
IDEOLOGY AND MOTIVATION

People who fought in the LPR's armed formations could be categorised into three main groups. The first and most important group numerically were locally recruited Donbas residents. Despite almost constant shortages of military personnel from 2014 to 2022, the LPR did not impose general conscription on its population until February 2022. During this period, the LPR relied on 'volunteers' only. The vast majority of individuals within the LPR's armed formations were from Donbas, and this remained the case even though the senior ranks were filled with Russian military officers to provide command and control.

International volunteers formed the second group, such individuals were especially prominent in the initial phases of the conflict in 2014 and 2015. One study suggested that '…perhaps about 50,000 people went through Donbas who were non-citizens of Ukraine, and out of them 30,000 were combatants. Many of them did not stay long—there were people who came for two weeks or a month… Their combat effectiveness mostly was not great, but they manned the ranks and generated a spirit of solidarity.'[1]

International volunteers were usually motivated by the ideology of the LPR and DPR, and the haphazard ideology the two People's Republics espoused allowed for a 'wide church' in which numerous international volunteers felt welcomed, ranging from Neo-Nazi to extreme left anti-Fascist individuals. 'Prizrak' for example had a 'Volunteer Communist Detachment' which attracted foreign volunteers under an 'anti-fascist' banner.

Their presence amongst the nascent armed formations of the LPR in 2014 and 2015 was usually far more important in terms of propaganda than actual fighting strength, and by the end of 2014, most international fighters had returned home. 'Most of the volunteer combatants left after the battle for Debaltseve in early 2015 … although those who wanted, stayed. Funding from their private benefactors subsided.'[2]

Russian Federation military personnel formed the third group, deployed to the LPR's armed formations to fill specialist support, command, and liaison roles. These were distinct from Russian military personnel who fought in Donbas in regular Russian Federation forces deployed to the region as discrete units, in particular during the 'Northern Wind', the covert large-scale Russian intervention in Ukraine that began in August 2014, and again in the massive 'special military operation' starting in February 2022.

From 2014 to 2022, this filling of LPR armed formation units with Russian military personnel was done covertly, but extensive OSINT research over the years exposed numerous Russian military personnel serving in the LPR's armed formations. For example, as examined in more detail below, it is thought that the LPR's 4th Separate Motorised Rifle Brigade's 3rd Motor Rifle Battalion 'Vityaz' was comprised primarily of Russian soldiers from the 15th

LPR militants patrolling near Luhansk, 2 July 2014. The vehicle is a modified UAZ-469 with flatbed rear and improvised armoured plates on the front. Mounted on the vehicle is an NSV 12.7mm heavy machinegun. (Associated Press/Alamy Stock Photo)

Separate Motorised Rifle "Peacekeeping" Brigade from the Russian Federation's Central Military District. Probably for this reason it kept a lower profile in public than its sister battalions in the same brigade, which were comprised mostly of Luhansk locals.

Overall it has been estimated that among the DPR and LPR's armed formations, in the early stages of the conflict '…about 50 percent of the fighters were local to Donbas, 30 percent came from the rest of Ukraine including its western part, 10 percent were from Russia, and 10 percent from a variety of other countries.'[3]

Foundation myths: Novorossiya and Russian Eurasianism

The armed formations of both the LPR and DPR fought under the flag of Novorossiya, and it is worth briefly examining this as a concept. Literally meaning 'New Russia', the word was historically used in the Russian Empire to denote the steppe lands annexed by Catherine the Great in the second half of the eighteenth century along the north shores of the Black Sea.

Novorossiya as a modern day political concept, and contrary to popular belief, '…was not invented by Putin after Crimea but emerged during the dissolution of the USSR. In Odesa, a "Democratic Union of Novorossiya" was established in 1991 and campaigned for a "special state status" within its historical boundaries. The idea did not presuppose joining Russia, but was a kind of new beginning for the lands that comprised it.'[4] In the early years after Ukrainian independence, such ideas gained little attention, and remained the preserve of a small group of political enthusiasts.

In neighbouring Donetsk oblast, the concept of the Donetsk-Krivoy Rog[5] Republic was resurrected after the fall of the Soviet Union. An organisation called the International Movement for Donbas was founded at Donetsk National University in the early 1990s, and campaigned for greater political autonomy for Donbas. Despite being censured by the Ukrainian authorities they continued working, but their beliefs and objectives remained very much at the fringe of Ukrainian politics until the events of 2014.

Novorossiya full colour flag patches, c. 2016. This were common patches worn by LPR militants even after the shelving of the Novorossiya confederation project between the LPR and DPR. (Private collection, used with permission, and Dean O'Brien collection)

Among its founding members was Vladimir Kornilov, a historian who in 2011 published a book called *Donetsk-Krivoy Rog Republic: The Assassinated Dream.*[6] The Russian Civil War-era Donetsk-Krivoy Rog Soviet Republic was a short-lived self-proclaimed Soviet Republic that existed for a short period in 1918 before vanishing. This book later became a key foundation stone in the national myth-making of the DPR.

In Russia, in the decade running up to 2014, the work of the Russian ideologue Aleksandr Dugin was quietly gaining traction. His work was a development on the theory of 'Eurasianism' which had been espoused by a Soviet writer called Lev Gumilev in the 1930s. Dugin developed these ideas into a neo-Eurasianism, which at its core saw Russia as a distinct cultural unit to the West.

As tensions with the West began to rise, the 'Eurasianist'

Novorossiya magnet, c. 2016. Previously fringe revanchist theories exploded to life in eastern Ukraine in 2014. (Private collection, used with permission)

idea started to influence the thinking of senior Russian leaders, allowing them to see Russia as '…occupying a pivotal position as an independent great power located astride both Europe and Asia.' This ambition gives rise to lies at the core of Putin's "Greater Eurasia" project, a still-inchoate and evolving mix of identity assertion, economic vehicle, and geopolitical construct.'[7] Eurasianism as a concept was also appealing to the Russian leadership as it espoused rejecting Western influences on 'traditional' Russian culture and values.

Dugin also eagerly resurrected the concept of Novorossiya to further his arguments: 'In 2009, in a nationalist prank, Dugin drew a map of a dismembered Ukraine, which included the fateful words 'Novorossiya' to signify the eastern provinces … His use of the tsarist-era term prefigured by five years Putin's use of the same label.'[8]

There is a lot of debate about Dugin and the extent to which he actually held any influence in the Kremlin. Nevertheless: 'Whether or not the Kremlin listens to Dugin, his views are of interest as a bellwether of intellectual opinion towards adapting Russia's imperial afterlife to the modern world.'[9]

The concept of Eurasianism now began to enter mainstream discourse in Russia, with Putin quoting from the theory of Eurasianism in a major speech in 2012. An idea that would '… previously, have been considered marginal and even barking mad were suddenly the anchor of … [Putin's] most important speech of the year. And these ideas would make themselves clearer 15 months later, when Russian soldiers … seized airports and … chokepoints across Crimea, starting a domino effect that would lead to war in eastern Ukraine.'[10]

Three Colours of Novorossiya

Three main strands of ideology underpinned the two People's Republics of eastern Ukraine, referred to by the historian Marlene Laruelle as the 'Three Colours of Novorossiya.' The three colours were red, white and brown.[11]

The red strand of ideology focused on glorification of the Soviet Union, which in the LPR was reflected in both the use of Soviet symbology, and emphasising the industrial legacy of the Donbas. This type of ideology was usually derided by detractors as 'neo-Soviet' owing to its use of Soviet symbols, many of which – such as the Order of Victory – related to the victory of the Soviet Union during the Second World War.

Other examples of neo-Soviet, 'red' ideology in the LPR and DPR focused on Stalin and his image as a powerful wartime leader. However, the use of neo-Soviet ideology by the People's Republics was limited and very selective – there never any real attempt to move back towards Soviet-style economic planning.

The white strand was based on the use of tsarist imagery, mixed in with ideas from Orthodox theocracy. This form of ideology was often openly religious, and espoused in phrases such as 'We are Russian – God is with us.' White strand ideology was usually linked to that of the 'Russian World' concept. 'Some researchers claim that it is a type of neo-imperialist strategy which aims to create an anti-Western and anti-democratic consolidation on the basis of the Orthodox denomination.'[12]

The brown ideological strand rested on the concept of the 'Russian Spring.' In terminology borrowed from the 'Arab Spring' it expressed itself in a desire for a culturally-Russian state, freed of Western influence, corruption, oligarchs, and moral decadence. This ideology often celebrated military activity and glorified violence, reflected in social media posts which detailed the exploits of LPR

Stalin patch, c. 2018. Depictions of Stalin formed a strand of 'red' ideology in the LPR and DPR, with the writing below reading 'Effective Manager!' (Private collection, used with permission)

Russian Imperial flag patches, widely available in the DPR and LPR c. 2016. The black, white and yellow flag was Russia's official flag from 1858 to 1896. Among LPR and DPR militants it saw a revival in the form of white strand ideology. The version with the motto states 'We are Russian – God is With Us' and was popular amongst troops opposed to communist ideals. (Private collection, used with permission, and Dean O'Brien collection)

White strand ideology in the form of an image of Christ, subdued and full colour patchs, c. 2017. Such images in patch or flag form were sometimes displayed by members of the LPR armed formations. It depicts the face of Christ and is known as the Gonfalon/Mandylion patch. It originates from the Orthodox icon 'Not Made By Hands' flag which is seen flying from many vehicles and hung in trenches in the current conflict. (Private collection, used with permission, and Dean O'Brien collection)

and DPR fighters, often accompanied by combat footage and martial music.

To an external observer, one immediately apparent aspect of these three 'colours' of LPR and DPR ideology is how contradictory they appear. As one such observer noted: 'While many Russian nationalists and imperialists draw on imagery from both the pre- and post-Revolutionary periods, tsarist symbols continue to be anathema to diehard Communists, while Communist symbols are abhorred by most Orthodox believers.'[13] In fact, this wide range of ideology allowed the LPR and DPR to draw in people with a wide range of beliefs to fight against the Ukrainian government.

Donbas identity

Another explanation of the ideological motivation of those who fought for the LPR places more emphasis on a localised 'Donbas identity' than ideologies connected with the wider 'Russian world'

concept. The 'Donbas identity' was thought to have developed from the heavy industrialisation of the region noted above, which created a strong identification with the Donbas region and its place in the Soviet Union – a state that vanished in 1991 – and only weak identification with Ukraine. In a pre-conflict 2007 study, it was suggested that '…one could describe most inhabitants of the Donetsk region as *tutoshnii*, that is, people whose main identification is with their locality rather than with the state or nation.'[14]

Notably, many early LPR militants were not necessarily intent on joining Russia immediately, but rather wanted to set Donbas on its own path. One study of attitudes in Donbas discovered that '… mistrust toward Moscow and Kyiv were present in nearly equal measure among the region's industrial workers in 2014.'[15]

From 2015 onwards, it was noted that the very existence of the two People's Republics in eastern Ukraine, owing to the failure of the Novorossiya 'confederation' project, also cast doubt on the political and ideological commitment to an over-arching 'Donbas identity.' Despite a looming existential threat from the Ukrainian state and its armed forces, the two People's Republics were unable or unwilling to form a single, coherent political entity – i.e. Novorossiya.

Economic motivations

An important motivator for many of the members of the LPR's armed formations was likely to have been economic rather than ideological. As explored above, the prestige of the Donbas's heavy industries such as manufacturing, coal mining and metal production was largely dependent on the region's important strategic position within the Russian Empire and then Soviet Union, and a decline in these heavy industries was already under way when the Soviet Union collapsed.

The economic decline in Donbas accelerated under independent Ukraine. Many of the coal mines – forming such an important part of the Donbas identity – had already been worked out, and many of the manufacturing industries were uncompetitive compared to other parts of the world. For many businesses, the start of the conflict in 2014 provided a final nail in the coffin, after which many of the major industrial concerns in the LPR were shuttered or worked only at minimal capacity. The famous Luhansk Locomotive Plant closed its doors for good in 2015, and the huge Alchevsk metal plant also effectively all but ceased operating in the same year.

In such an environment of high unemployment and lack of opportunities, a stable salary for serving in the armed formations of the LPR would have seemed attractive. A 2021 social media advert for service in the LPR 6th Separate Motorised Rifle Cossack Regiment offered a salary of 16,500 roubles (approximately $230 at the time), plus 2 percent extra for each day undertaking a combat mission, and a full clothing and food allowance. Joining the LPR's armed formations may have been the only attractive option for many individuals, given the lack of any employment elsewhere. This lack of alternatives was possibly in many cases a stronger motivating factor than any ideology.

Conclusion

In the early stages of the conflict in Luhansk in 2014, the early armed formations of the LPR were able to attract fighters from a wide range of background, motivated by a very diverse range of ideological factors. The situation in the DPR was similar, with Igor 'Strelkov' Girkin noting there that: 'The irregular army gathers individuals of different opinions, united by a common Russian language and hatred against Ukraine. It is injurious for our common deal to create any common ideology for them.'[16]

Unlike the neighbouring DPR however, the LPR had much less of a coherent ideology and no historical 'forebear' (however historically tenuous) to base their foundation myth on. The presence of numerous groups claiming Cossack origins, which will be discussed below, was another factor, with many of these groups initially strongly and sometimes violently opposed to the LPR leadership in Luhansk. This lack of a coherent ideology manifested itself in the chaos and infighting within the LPR after 2014, as various factions with vastly differing ideology and objectives struggled for power.

3
PROPAGANDA AND SYMBOLOGY

As discussed in the previous chapter, the lack of a single unifying ideology was one of the main issues that the LPR was forced to contend with. This mirrored what has been called the 'ideological vacuum' at the heart of Russia following the collapse of the Soviet Union. The LPR, like the Kremlin, settled upon the memory of the Second World War, and the glory and military might of the Soviet Union during that conflict, as a useful ideological tool by which to unite the populace under its control.

As in Russia and the DPR, a particularly important celebration in the LPR calendar was the 9 May Victory parade, held annually in central Luhansk. During these parades, tens of thousands of people lined the streets to see LPR militants marching past, followed by columns of LPR armoured fighting vehicles, artillery and other military equipment. Huge screens displayed videos that seamlessly mixed Soviet symbology from the Second World War with contemporary LPR symbols. In this way, '…Propaganda … created in people's minds a virtual continuation of the Great Patriotic War in the shape of the war in the Donbass; where the Ukrainians have been given the role of the fascists.'[1]

Flags

The LPR's armed formations fought under and displayed two flags, that of Novorossiya, and that of the LPR itself. Designed in 2013 by pro-Russian activists, the Novorossiya flag was in 2014 often the only insignia to be seen on the uniforms of many militants. Dugin, the Russian Eurasianist ideologue, supposedly '… correctly predicted the design of the flag … red with a blue St Andrew's cross – two months before a contest was held to decide it.'[2]

The LPR flag was invented after the events of early 2014, as there was no equivalent to the historical research and political irredentism that had been developed in Donetsk. Indeed, at some of the early violent protests and storming of Ukrainian government buildings in Luhansk, it was the DPR flag that was flown, alongside those of Russia.

'The LNR flag had no prior history and was designed from scratch. Communism-era references were important at the LNR, and its symbolic reflected that, while the place of religion was low-key. Its flag prominently featured the five-point star relating the new "republic" to its Soviet

LPR flag full colour patch. This depicts the third iteration of the LPR flag, used around 2017–2020. A simpler version in the form of a simpler tricolour became the preferred version later, worn by LPR militants during the full-scale invasion of 2022. (Private collection, used with permission)

An LPR dugout with the flag of the LPR displayed, 3 February 2022. The snow camouflage overcoat is based on the *klyaksa* (ink blot) pattern. (Abaca Press/Alamy Stock Photo)

heritage supplemented by a small eight-point Orthodox star in its coats of arms.'[3] The flag went through several design iterations, becoming plainer until it was a simple tricolour of pale blue, dark blue and red.

Subdued versions of the Novorossiya and LPR flags were sometimes seen on the combat uniforms of LPR armed formation militants. Full-coloured patches were mainly used for parades or by non-frontline units. Cossack units present in the LPR, often wore or flew the flag of the Don Cossack Host, blue-yellow-red.

St. George's Ribbon

The St. George's ribbon was another very common piece of symbology, especially during the early days of the conflict during which it was perhaps the only symbol common across both DPR and LPR militants. Despite having historical roots, the St. George's ribbon was a relatively 'new' piece of symbology that originated in Russia in 2005. 'The ribbon is modelled on a high-ranking order instituted by the Stalin regime in 1942. It has the same colours as the Soviet medal but a different name: the Soviet prototype was called 'Order of the Guard' (*gvardeiskii orden*) … Both the Order itself as well as various kinds of ornamentation in orange and black featured on numerous wartime and post-war posters and postcards.'[4]

In early 2014 the ribbon seemed to emerge as an identifying symbol for the early armed formations of the LPR and DPR. Among the LPR militants standing guard outside the Ukrainian government buildings they had just stormed, the St. George's ribbon was often the only unifying symbol on their motley collection of partial uniforms and civilian dress.

Artem Shevchenko, a Ukrainian journalist who was in Donbas in the early days of the conflict, wrote: 'There were separatists' paraphernalia in almost every town, such as notorious brown-and-black St. George's ribbons, Russian tricolors, black-blue-and-red flags of the still to be proclaimed "Donetsk People's Republic", and other symbols of different illegal groups operating in the region.'[5] Such was its association with separatism that the production and display of such ribbons was quickly banned in Ukraine.[6]

Along with the Novorossiya flag, the St George's ribbon was one of a couple of symbols universally adopted across both of the People's

Two variations of the St. George's ribbon patch, Donbas c. 2016. (Private collection, used with permission, and Dean O'Brien collection)

Republics in eastern Ukraine, helping to bind together numerous highly ideologically diverse groups.

4

STRATEGIC AIMS OF THE LPR AND THE RUSSIAN FEDERATION

Though commonly described as having 'separatist' aspirations, in fact the strategic aims of the LPR as an entity were broader and sometimes highly contradictory. This reflected the manner in which the LPR had been formed, and the wide range of political viewpoints held by its political elite and military commanders.

In fact a number of strategic goals were mooted over the years by the LPR and its principle actors, which included autonomy as an independent state, a desire for complete annexation by Russia (in the manner of Crimea), and reincorporation into Ukraine as an autonomous entity under a federalised political system.

The effective federalisation of Ukraine was in fact one of the aims of the Minsk II ceasefire agreement, and was probably more in line with Russian foreign policy objectives at the beginning of the conflict in 2014. Within a federalised Ukraine, autonomous and pro-Kremlin administrations in Donetsk and Luhansk oblast

would have been able to stymie Ukrainian moves towards closer integration with the EU and NATO.

In general, in the years between 2014 and 2022, the LPR claimed to be fighting for control of all the territory within the boundaries of Luhansk oblast, a goal stated by numerous early LPR armed formation commanders, many of whom opposed the brokered Minsk ceasefire as the LPR had only captured around 30 percent of the pre-conflict oblast.

However, when large-scale Russian military support was withdrawn from Luhansk oblast after the 'Northern Wind' of mid-2014 to early 2015, the LPR lacked sufficient combat power to do much more than hold the existing contact line running through the oblast, and solidify its positions within the territory it controlled. It was only with the massive full-scale Russian invasion of Ukraine in

2022 that the LPR was finally able to realise its objective of reaching the boundaries of Luhansk oblast.

Russian strategic goals in Donbas

There is a lot of debate about the extent to which Russian involvement in Donbas in 2014 was part of a calculated Kremlin strategy to dismember Ukraine, or, at the other end of the spectrum, the result of becoming involved in a conflict that Kremlin propaganda had helped to ignite and could then not let fail.

Though the Kremlin gave some hesitant initial support to the uprisings in Donetsk and Luhansk, the Crimea scenario hoped for by many of those occupying government buildings and fighting Ukrainian forces in eastern Ukraine in early 2014, involving large-scale deployment of Russian Federation forces and subsequent complete annexation did not occur.

Later in 2014, faced with the prospect of the total military defeat of the DPR and LPR, the Kremlin committed significant ground forces to eastern Ukraine to inflict a series of defeats on Ukrainian forces, notably at Ilovaisk. Despite this, the Kremlin still refused to recognise either the LPR or DPR, or to immediately and completely annex them as it had done with Crimea. Faced with the intransigence of the two People's Republics, and their refusal to merge with each other politically or militarily, it also quietly dropped public support for the 'Novorossiya' confederation project as well.

Publicly, the Kremlin expressed support for the Minsk agreements signed in 2014 and 2015, but also positioned itself as an external actor, clinging to an increasingly flimsy claim of non-involvement in the conflict. As the fighting continued along the contact line in the years between 2015 and 2022, Putin maintained that the causes of the conflict were '...rooted in long-simmering discontent in the Donbass and social and political cleavages within modern Ukraine.'[1]

Again, this brings the discussion back to whether Russian involvement in Donbas was part of some pre-planned grand strategy, or a series of improvisations seeking to make the best of a situation largely of the Kremlin's own making. By fanning the flames of separatism in eastern and southern Ukraine in 2014, the Kremlin had raised expectations among many pro-Russian Ukrainians there that they would support them fully.

But when the expected 'People's Republics' in other key Ukrainian cities like Odesa and Kharkiv either failed to materialise or were swiftly snuffed out in early 2014, the Kremlin evidently decided against a larger scale incursion into Ukraine, providing limited equipment and support to the nascent DPR and LPR forces, but otherwise leaving them to fend for themselves.

In light of the massive Russian 'special military operation' into Ukraine in February 2022, it is perhaps easy to assume that the stated or eventual goals of that assault were the Kremlin's strategic plan all along. The writer Tony Wood suggests that in the years since 2008, the Kremlin's aggressive military interventions abroad in Ukraine and Syria have been '...largely improvised, focused on short-term tactical thinking rather than any longer-term project. The apparent aggression stems not from a growing confidence, but from a pervasive and deepening anxiety about Russian weakness.'[2]

It is also highly likely that different factions within the Kremlin pursued different aims for eastern Ukraine over the years following 2014. A hard-line faction wanted to keep the territories wrested from Ukraine in Donbas permanently. Another faction, with an eye on the biting sanctions and worsening relationships with the West, wanted to push for the fulfilment of the Minsk agreements. In the years between 2015 and 2022, it was likely that it was the latter option was predominant in Kremlin strategic thinking, and that in Donbas 'Moscow's ultimate political goal there is to insert the 'rebel republics' back into the fabric of the Ukrainian state while maintaining full control over them. This would force Kiev to accept the rebel territories' de facto right of veto over Ukrainian policy.'[3]

As late as January 2021, when a 'Russia Donbas Forum' on the future of the region was held in DPR-held Donetsk, 'Putin was not there, and his press secretary later distanced the Kremlin from the event, saying that integrating the Donbas into Russia was not a policy worth pursuing.'[4]

By 2022, it must have been evident to the Kremlin, that this strategy had failed. Despite the simmering conflict in Donbas, Ukraine was continuing full speed on its path towards Euro-Atlantic integration. The strategy was then changed to one in which full-scale military force would be brought to bear on Ukraine. The DPR and LPR were both formally annexed by Russia on 30 September 2022, almost eight and a half years after they had proclaimed their independence.

5
KEY BATTLES AND FORMATION OF LPR UNITS

This section will outline some of the key battles that took place during the creation of the LPR, and with them the creation of some of the LPR's armed formations. The role of the Cossacks in the LPR's armed formations will also be examined.

Events in Luhansk (March – May 2014)

Events in Luhansk oblast took a similar pattern to those in neighbouring Donetsk, starting with the violent seizures of government buildings, and large crowds gathering to proclaim hitherto relatively obscure individuals as the leaders of new political entities. Out of these groups of violent protestors in Luhansk in March and April of 2014 came the nucleus of many of the future armed formation units of what would become the LPR's 2nd Army Corps.

On 5 March 2014, following the example set in Donetsk by the 'election' of Pavel Gubarev four days earlier, crowds gathered in front of the Luhansk oblast administration building in central Luhansk to proclaim Aleksandr Kharitonov as the 'People's Governor.'

A few days later on 9 March 2014, the Luhansk oblast administration building was stormed and occupied by violent protestors. However, Ukrainian security forces were at this time still present in force in Luhansk, despite the worsening situation, and Kharitonov was arrested. Later, he was exchanged in a prisoner swap, later returning to Luhansk and joining the Cossack National Guard.

Masked LPR militants at the barricaded entrance to the Luhansk regional administration building, 30 April 2014. They both carry AK-74 5.45mm assault rifles. (Cosimo Attanasio/Alamy Stock Photo)

On 6 April 2014, thousands of violent protestors stormed the Luhansk headquarters of the Ukrainian State Security Services (SBU), seizing numerous weapons there and erecting barricades to try and prevent government forces from retaking the building. Among the protestors were around 50 men formerly of the Berkut riot police, now calling themselves the 'Army of the South-East.'[1] In these chaotic days, numerous armed and violent groups sprang up across Donbas, calling themselves a 'battalion,' 'brigade,' or even 'army' with little or no relation to their actual size.

The protestors refused to recognise the legitimacy of the new Ukrainian government in Kyiv, and were also calling for a referendum on the future of Donetsk and Luhansk to be held on 11 May 2014. The Luhansk SBU headquarters was recaptured by Ukrainian forces on 12 April 2014, but it was clear that the security situation in eastern Ukraine was rapidly deteriorating.

On 21 April 2014 there was another massive protest outside the Luhansk oblast administration building, with protestors electing Valery Bolotov as the 'People's Governor' and for the federalisation of Ukraine. The Ukrainian prosecutor's office immediately denounced these demands as separatist, and also noted that the flag of the DPR was being flown at the rallies.[2] The DPR had the advantage of its ideology having being developed over a decade in advance, there was no such equivalent in the LPR and it would have to be invented later.

Events were now accelerating, another rally on 27 April 2014 protestors proclaimed the 'Luhansk People's Republic' and warned the Ukrainian government that an armed insurgency would take place if their demands, including that for a referendum on the status of Luhansk oblast, were not met.

When these demands were not responded to, on 29 April 2014 thousands of violent protestors stormed the Luhansk oblast administration building, as well as other government offices. Some were carrying weapons seized from government forces, many wielded more primitive weapons like wooden clubs.

Elsewhere in Luhansk oblast, government buildings were being seized by protestors, in an uncoordinated fashion. On 29 April 2014, the government administration building in Pervomaisk was seized, on the same day the Alchevsk administration building was stormed by 30 militants who took down the Ukrainian flag.[3] Militants from the 'Army of the South-East' seized the district police station in Slovianoserbsk on 1 May 2014.

Start of the ATO and the Ukrainian recapture of Sloviansk (April 2014)

On 16 April 2014, the Ukrainian interim government launched an Anti-Terrorist Operation (ATO) in Donbas, in order to reassert control over the two oblasts. The initial Ukrainian offensive was plagued by a lack of readiness among the regular military, which had been starved of funding in the years since independence, as well as command and control problems.

Nevertheless, the armoured infantry units of the Ukrainian armed forces, backed by airpower in the form of ground attack jets and attack helicopters, began to make progress against the still relatively lightly armed militants of the DPR and LPR. By early May 2014, Igor 'Strelkov' Girkin and his forces in the DPR were facing a mechanised Ukrainian onslaught against their stronghold of Sloviansk in Donetsk oblast, which had been one of the first cities in Donbas to be captured by DPR forces.

Furthermore, the LPR uprising had not seen much success in northern Luhansk oblast, where the communities were smaller and there was much less pro-Russian sentiment. Additionally, Ukrainian forces still held numerous key sites across Luhansk oblast, including Luhansk Airport and much of the border with Russia.

LPR referendum (May 2014)

On 11 May 2014, a referendum on the status of the LPR was held, on the same day as a similar referendum in territory controlled by the DPR. The protestors storming government buildings in April had been demanding a referendum on being annexed by Russia, but the Kremlin was not keen to back this, so the wording settled upon was instead more ambiguous, the Russian word used meaning either 'self-rule' or 'independence.'

The referendum was overwhelmingly in favour of 'independence.' Aside from the obvious LPR control over the whole referendum process, the vote probably nevertheless did to a certain degree reflect the popular will of those who actually voted – any pro-Ukrainian citizen living in an area where the referendum was held would most likely have boycotted the illegitimate process.

As a result of the referendum, on 12 May 2014 Valery Bolotov '…showed up on the stage in [the] center of Luhansk, surrounded by two men armed with Kalashnikovs. He greeted a crowd by proclaiming the creation of an independent Luhansk Republic based on the results of Sunday's referendum, which is illegal under Ukrainian law.'[4]

A day later, Bolotov was wounded in an assassination attempt in which unidentified attackers shot at his car. He then went across to Russia for medical treatment, but when crossing back into Ukraine, was arrested by Ukrainian border guards.

During this period, much of the Russia-Ukraine border in Luhansk oblast was still, despite its porous nature, under the control

Valery Bolotov (centre), greets people in central Luhansk city as they declare independence for the Luhansk region, 12 May 2014. The orange and black flags of the 'Army of the South-East' are prominently displayed to the left of the picture. (Associated Press/Alamy Stock Photo)

of the Ukrainian government. Reportedly, around 200 armed militants from the 'Army of the South-East' then drove to the border checkpoint and, after a firefight against the vastly outnumbered border guards, secured Bolotov's release.[5]

Fighting in Luhansk (June 2014)

In the early hours of the morning on 2 June 2014, a large force of around 100 LPR militants attacked a Ukrainian Border Guard headquarters buildings on the outskirts of the city, using small arms and RPGs.[6] A single Ukrainian jet was sent to support the Border Guards defending the headquarters, but was unable to properly target the LPR militants as they were firing from inside and

between residential buildings. By daybreak, the number of militants attacking the headquarters had risen to around 500, and eventually the Ukrainian Border Guards had to surrender and withdraw.

On the same day, 2 June, a series of explosions hit the Luhansk oblast administration building and its vicinity, killing eight civilians.[7] The LPR blamed the Ukrainians for launching an airstrike, the Ukrainian authorities in turn blamed a misfired LPR anti-aircraft system.

The event shocked the inhabitants of the city. Most Luhansk residents believed it to have been caused by a Ukrainian airstrike, the first time civilians had been killed in such a manner since the start of the conflict. For the LPR, it allowed them to build on the narrative that the new post-Maidan government in Kyiv was attacking its own people in Donbas.

LPR withdrawal from northern Luhansk oblast (June – August 2014)

Despite setbacks in Luhansk itself, by June 2014, the Ukrainian ATO counter-offensive was making progress and reversing territorial gains made by the LPR's armed formations in Luhansk, in particular in the northern half of the oblast.

The LPR lost control of Shchastia on the Siverskyi Donets River in June 2014, as Ukrainian forces from the 'Aidar' volunteer battalion pushed LPR militants from the city. This was a major blow as the gigantic Luhansk Thermal Power Plant was located there, providing electricity to much of the oblast. Ukrainian forces also established a tiny bridgehead on the south side of the H21 highway bridge crossing the Siverskyi Donets, which became for many years the only Ukrainian presence on the south side of the river in relative proximity to the city of Luhansk.

Under Igor Girkin's orders, LPR forces including some Cossack units and 'Prizrak' battalion were forced to withdraw from the Lysychansk-Sievierodonetsk-Rubizhne triangle of industrial cities in July 2014, retreating south to consolidate their positions. In a similar manner to the DPR's loss of Mariupol in 2014, this

An LPR militant fires his AK-74 5.45mm assault rifle during clashes with Ukrainian Border Guard troops on the outskirts of Luhansk, 2 June 2014. Several hundred LPR militants attacked a Ukrainian Border Guard base in Luhansk, with some firing rocket-propelled grenades from the roof of a nearby residential building. (Associated Press/Alamy Stock Photo)

Monument to the civilians killed in the 2 June 2014 explosions in central Luhansk, attributed by the LPR to a Ukrainian airstrike. (PLPK Stock Photo)

An LPR militant at an improvised road block in Stanitsya Luhanska, 17 June 2014. (Credit: Igor Golovnov / Alamy Stock Photo)

Around the same time, to the west in Donetsk oblast, Ukrainian forces had reached Ilovaisk and were threatening to encircle the DPR-held oblast capital of Donetsk. Igor 'Strelkov' Girkin, who had been so instrumental in lighting the flames of conflict in Donbas, loudly and publicly appealed for more Russian aid. For the Kremlin, the spectre of the total military defeat of the DPR and LPR loomed.

The Kremlin realised it had to urgently replace the Russian-born DPR and LPR leaders with Ukrainian-born individuals. 'By August [2014], it was clear the separatists were on the precipice of failure, and a negotiated settlement with Ukraine would prove difficult to orchestrate given that the leaders of the separatist republics were both Russian citizens (i.e., externally introduced actors who could not negotiate on behalf of the breakaway regions). In effect, the facade of a locally inspired rebellion became pointless.'[9]

On 14 August 2014 in the LPR, Valery Bolotov, who had been born in Taganrog in Russia, was replaced as head of the LPR by Igor Plotnitsky, a Ukrainian. This mirrored similar rapid changes in the DPR, where Igor 'Strelkov' Girkin resigned on the same day and was recalled to Russia, and Alexander Borodai had been replaced by the Donbas-born Alexander Zakharchenko as Prime Minister of the DPR

was a major blow for the LPR's future as a coherent economic unit, as much of Luhansk's industry was located in these three cities.

By August 2014, Ukrainian forces were clearing LPR militants from the town of Stanytsia Luhanska on the northern bank of the Siverskyi Donets River. Along with Shchastia, Stanytsia Luhanska was one of the two major crossing points across the river in eastern Luhansk oblast, and the bridges (one road and one rail) across the river were only 15km from the centre of Luhansk city. By mid-August, the '...LNR was in a really bad shape [...] The ATO troops laid a siege on Luhansk and seized some ground inside the city on August 18; they were also completing their maneuver to isolate and block Alchevsk defended by *Prizrak*, and occupied the villages nearby. Rebels still fought for Luhansk and Stanitsa Luhanska under ... unrelenting artillery fire.'[8]

on 7 August 2014.

Direct Russian intervention into Luhansk (August 2014)

Owing to the deteriorating situation for its two proxy forces in eastern Ukraine, the Kremlin now chose to act more openly, and committed significant ground forces. On 19 August the so-called 'Northern Wind' operation started, in which LPR forces began a counter-offensive backed by Russian ground forces including armour and artillery.

Satellite imagery released by NATO showed columns of Russian armour and self-propelled artillery moving through Sorokyne (formerly Krasnodon) in Luhansk oblast, southwest of the Luhansk city itself.[10] The Russians were also targeting Ukrainian forces with cross-border artillery fire originating from inside Russia itself.

Igor Plotnitsky, head of the Luhansk People's Republic, gives an interview to journalists in Luhansk city centre, October 2014. A member of his security detail behind him carries an AK-74 5.45mm assault rifle. (Iva Zimova/Panos Pictures)

A key target for the combined LPR and Russian forces was Luhansk Airport, where Ukrainian forces, including the 80th Airborne Brigade, had held out in a 'pocket' south of Luhansk city since April 2014. The airport had been the scene of one of the worst single losses of life for the Ukrainian armed forces in the first year of the conflict, when an Il-76 transport plane was shot down by the LPR on 14 June 2014, killing 49 Ukrainian service personnel onboard.[11]

The airport was now attacked by Russian tanks supported by LPR militants. After heavy fighting, resulting in the almost complete destruction of the airport itself, the remaining Ukrainian forces withdrew on 1 September 2014, after 146 days of defence.[12]

In Luhansk oblast, the Russian military intervention of August and September 2014 helped to stabilise the territory the LPR already controlled, as well as eliminating remaining 'pockets' of Ukrainian control, primarily at Luhansk Airport. To the southwest, the DPR was also saved from defeat by the 'Northern Wind.' It also compelled Ukraine to sign the first Minsk agreement, on 5 September 2014.

Creation of LPR 2nd Army Corps (October 2014)

After the first Minsk agreement, the Kremlin began the first round of reorganisation, bringing the LPR's various 'battalions' and 'brigades' into a new creation, the LPR 2nd Army Corps. On 7 October 2014, the 'Army of the South-East' was transformed into the People's Militia of the LPR, and various battalions and separate units were merged into the brigades of the LPR 2nd Army Corps. This was only the beginning of a process that would take several years, with the aim of bringing fighting units in LPR under a single military command.

Civilians gather to look at a tank parked in Teatralnaya Ploshchad (Theatre Square) on the day before parliamentary elections for the Luhansk People's Republic in November 2014. The tank is a T-72B main battle tank, which the LPR started to receive from June 2014 onwards, but there is no tactical marking to denote which unit the tank belonged to. The LPR crewmember standing on the turret wears a Novorossiya flag patch on his arm while another crewmember is uncovering the NSVT 12.7mm heavy machine gun mounted on the commander's cupola. Elsewhere in the picture, a statue of Lenin is still standing in the square on the far left. (Iva Zimova/Panos Pictures)

Capture of Debaltseve (January – February 2015)

By January 2015, the Ukrainian Armed Forces in Debaltseve were surrounded on three sides by DPR armed formations to the west and south, and the armed formations of the LPR to the east. A small city largely built around a significant railway junction, Ukrainian control of Debaltseve formed a 'salient' into DPR and LPR-controlled territory, as well as sitting astride important communication routes between the DPR and LPR.

On 22 January 2015, the combined forces of the DPR and LPR, backed by regular Russian military units, commenced a concerted effort to capture Debaltseve. Russian support included artillery support, tanks, as well as more specialist support. R-330Zh Zhitel electronic warfare systems jammed Ukrainian communications, hampering the Ukrainian defence of the city. The city had been heavily fortified by the Ukrainian military, but now faced a co-ordinated attack from three sides. Six hundred militants from the Cossack National Guard reportedly played an important role in the fighting, as did elements of the LPR battalion 'Prizrak'.

Despite the signing of the Minsk II agreement on 12 February 2015, which aimed at stopping the fighting in Donbas, fierce fighting continued in Debaltseve.[13] The DPR leader Zakharchenko, who considered the Minsk agreements a 'betrayal', claimed that the Minsk II agreement did not apply to Debaltseve in order to keep DPR and LPR forces engaged there. On 18 February 2015, Debaltseve was finally captured by the combined forces of the DPR, LPR and Russian ground forces, and the remaining Ukrainian units were forced to withdraw to the northwest.

Role of Cossacks in the creation of the LPR's armed formations (2014)

One of the key differences between the formation of the LPR 2nd Army Corps in comparison to the DPR 1st Army Corps was the presence in Luhansk oblast in 2014 of a number of sizeable Cossack forces, which were only integrated into the LPR 2nd Army Corps with some difficulty.

These Cossack forces controlled huge swathes of Luhansk oblast nominally under the control of the LPR. 'In 2014 up to 60 percent of LNR territory was controlled by the fighters who identified themselves as Cossacks and served under their own atamans and also at *Prizrak* […] They were associated with lawlessness, courage and shortage of combat skills.'[14] Furthermore as one analyst noted, these groups, '…self-styled as Russian Cossacks, have divided up most of the "republic's" territory, defying the "central" leadership. Each one of those formations is entrenched in a specific territory and loyal to its own "ataman" (leader). They rarely cooperate with Luhansk or even among themselves.'[15]

Heavily romanticised in both Ukrainian and Russian culture, the Cossacks played an important role in both Russian Imperial and then Soviet military history. Historically, the Cossacks were recruited by the Russian and Soviet authorities as irregular cavalry soldiers, before being heavily suppressed by Stalin after the Second World War. It was only in the final years of the Soviet Union that the Cossacks were able to revive themselves as cultural groups and openly practice their traditions.

Arranged into 'hosts', it was the Don Cossack Host (Донское казачье войско) that existed as a semi-autonomous cultural group across the territory of what is now the Donbas region of Ukraine and neighbouring areas in Russia from the seventeenth century to the Russian Revolution of 1917. During the Russian Civil War, and in a similar manner to the Ukrainian nation to the west, the Don Cossacks experienced a brief period as an independent nation

Nikolai Kozitsyn, leader of the 'Cossack National Guard,' speaking to the press on 5 November 2014 in Perevalsk, Luhansk oblast. Behind him the flag of the 'Cossack National Guard' is displayed. (Associated Press/Alamy Stock Photo)

Don Cossack Host full colour patch, c. 2017. The blue, yellow and red colours of the flag date to 1918, when the flag was inaugurated in the short-lived Don Republic during the Russian Civil War. The Don Cossack coat of arms in the centre, depicting a white stag pierced by an arrow, is much older and dates back several centuries. (Private collection, used with permission)

by proclaiming a Don Republic with its capital at Novocherkassk in 1918. Allying with the White forces in the Civil War, they were defeated by the Red Army, and their culture heavily suppressed in the following decades.

Revived as a grouping from the late 1980s onwards, elements of the Don Cossacks played a central role in the fighting against the Ukrainian government in Luhansk oblast in 2014. The *ataman* (leader) of the International Union of Public Associations 'The Great Don Army,' Nikolai Kozitsyn, issued an appeal in late April 2014 calling for the creation of a 'Cossack National Guard' to fight Ukrainian forces in south-eastern Ukraine, '…consisting not only of participants in the Kiev Maidan and guys from western Ukraine, but also mercenaries from Europe and America.'[16] In effect he created a private armed formation, the 'Cossack National Guard,' which by 3

May 2014 was occupying Ukrainian government buildings in the city of Antratsyt in Luhansk oblast.[17]

The Cossacks raised the historical blue-yellow-red flag of the Don Cossack Army over captured government buildings, but it was notable that other parts of the Don Cossack movement in Russia disassociated themselves with the 'Cossack National Guard' and its presence in Ukraine.[18] One analyst noted that: 'This National Guard was meant … to receive non-registered Russian Cossacks as members—i.e., those not descended from the registered Cossacks of the Tsarist era … Unregistered Cossacks is a dubious status, often accessible to all comers. Most Cossacks in the "LPR," therefore, are probably less than authentic or not authentic at all.'[19]

Though the Cossack National Guard had taken up arms against the Ukrainian government, the aims of many of the Cossack military commanders ran counter to both that of the LPR and the LPR's Russian benefactor. This was because many of the Cossacks also viewed the nascent LPR itself '…as a "usurper" on the purported land of (Russian) Don Cossacks in Luhansk. These atamans claim to operate "Cossack self-administration"—in effect, their own personalized rule—in their respective portions of "LPR's" territory. And they aspire to merge that territory informally with the Don Cossacks' heartland in Russia's Rostov oblast.'[20]

From May till July 2014, the Cossack National Guard held positions in the heavily industrialised group of cities in western Luhansk oblast formed by the Lysychansk-Sievierodonetsk-Rubizhne triangle. During this time, they subordinated themselves not to the LPR leadership, but to that of Igor 'Strelkov' Girkin. Despite this, however, Strelkov assessed the overall combat performance of the Cossack units as poor.[21]

Estimates of their strength at this time were around 2,000–3,000 militants. As the Ukrainian ATO counter-offensive of mid-2014 got underway, the Cossack forces were forced to withdraw from the Lysychansk-Sievierodonetsk-Rubizhne triangle, after suffering heavy casualties.

Kozitsyn withdrew his remaining forces south, and set up headquarters in Antratsyt. His Cossack units also '…controlled long sections of … the Ukrainian side of the Russia-Ukraine border and the access routes into "LPR's" interior.'[22]

In addition to the Cossack National Guard (by far the largest of the Cossack armed formations), another notable unit was that led by a Pavel Dremov, named the 'First Cossack Regiment' of the Don Cossack Host. It was '…named after a legendary Don Cossack ataman Matvei Platov. It numbered 1,176 by January 1, 2015, according to the LNR "ministry of defence."'[23] Dremov apparently split his unit off from the Cossack National Guard, and moved to Kadiivka (formerly Stakhanov, Dremov's home town) over which he took control.[24]

Another Cossack commander was Yevgeny Ishchenko, an ataman who took control of the frontline city of Pervomaisk. Quoted in January 2015, Cossack militants in Pervomaisk believed that the lack of humanitarian aid from the LPR central authorities was owing to '…a deliberate policy to kill off the city through cold and hunger, the same as other areas with Cossack self-government. The … towns of Pervomaisk, Kirovsk, Stakhanov and Bryanka are under the control of armed men who proclaim themselves to be 'Cossack units' intent on creating 'true people's power.'[25]

By late 2014, both Kozitsyn and Dremov were publicly clashing with the LPR leader Igor Plotnitsky. Dremov was calling for the creation of a 'Cossack People's Republic' in Luhansk oblast, and was reluctant to recognise the LPR as an entity. Like Zakharchenko in neighbouring Donetsk oblast, he considered the Minsk ceasefire

agreements of late 2014 to be illegitimate, and called for a continuation of the conflict to the borders of Luhansk oblast.

Eventually it was decided to remove Kozitsyn, in this case quite literally. 'In late November [2014], another Cossack unit (believed to be undercover Spetsnaz) raided Kozitsyn's headquarters, killed his two closest aides and other retainers in a shootout, and removed the ataman forcibly to Russia.'[26]

Dremov was killed in a targeted assassination on 5 December 2014, a car bomb killing him on the day after his wedding as he drove between Stakhanov and Pervomaisk in Luhansk oblast. Though the LPR blamed a Ukrainian sabotage group, the press secretary of the Ministry of Internal Affairs of Ukraine, Artem Shevchenko, suggested that: 'the death of Dremov, as well as the previous leaders of terrorists in the "LPR" (Bednov, Ishchenko, Mozgovoi) could be the result of disputes between uncontrolled Cossack leaders and their Russian handlers.'[27]

Following the death of Dremov and the removal of Kozitsyn, after which many Cossacks left for Russia, the remnants of the 'Cossack National Guard' and 'First Cossack Regiment' were incorporated into the LPR 2nd Army Corps.

Minsk II and the reorganisation of the LPR's armed formations (early 2015)

Debaltseve represented the last major battle in the first two years of the conflict in eastern Ukraine, and as such the last large-scale change in the 'contact line' which now divided the two sides.

Calling for an immediate ceasefire from midnight on 15 February 2015, the Minsk II agreement committed both sides to withdraw their heavy military equipment from the contact line. Building upon Minsk I, it created designated buffer zones from which certain types of armour and artillery had to be withdrawn. A withdrawal zone 50km wide was created for artillery systems of 100mm calibre or greater, a zone 70km wide for MLRS (Grad-type multiple launch rocket system), and wider still for more powerful rocket and missile systems such as the 9P140 Uragan 220mm MLRS, 9K58 Smerch 300mm, and 9K79 Tochka-U. The LPR never fully implemented this withdrawal, and there were disagreements about where the withdrawal lines were, as the agreements had been drawn up while Debaltseve was still under the control of the Ukrainian armed forces.

With the capture of Debaltseve, the Kremlin realised that the LPR and DPR's armed formations would have to be reorganised. One stipulation of the Minsk agreements was the eventual political reintegration of the DPR and LPR into Ukraine. This suited the Kremlin, as it would allow them de facto veto control over Ukrainian foreign policy via their proxies.

However, the LPR had a number of unruly battalion commanders, many of whom, such as Dremov, opposed Minsk and wanted to keep fighting. In addition, many of the same battalion commanders barely recognised the authority of the central LPR government in Luhansk, and ran their own personal fiefdoms in the cities they controlled. 'Alchevsk was ruled by Alexei Mozgovoi whereas in Stakhanov, it was Pavel Dremov. Pervomaisk was under the leadership of Russian Cossacks and Krasnyi Luch was led by Anatoly Kozitsyn, the self-proclaimed ataman from Novocherkassk.'[28]

Owing to the influence of Igor 'Strelkov' Girkin in Donetsk, and a marginally more coherent uniting ideology, the DPR was easier to reform in this manner. In the LPR, the situation was more complicated by the more fragmented units, the presence of Cossack formations, and a generally less coherent overall ideology.

In March 2015, a series of interim reorganisations began. While the main line brigades of LPR 2nd Army Corps had already been

An LPR T-64B tank on the move outside Luhansk city, 21 February 2015. This T-64 has been fitted with Kontakt-1 ERA blocks in an improvised and non-standard pattern, with the blocks around the turret fixed on horizontally rather than vertically. A light snow camouflage spray-paint coat has also been applied. (Associated Press/Alamy Stock Photo)

formed, some of the high-profile battalions with intransigent commanders were now designated as Territorial Defence Battalions.

There then also followed a series of targeted assassinations against a number of LPR battalion commanders and other prominent political figures, such as the killing of Mozgovoi, leader of 'Prizrak' on 23 May 2015.

'Frozen' conflict (February 2015 – February 2022)

After Debaltseve, the contact line remained frozen for almost seven years. An uneasy and often violent stalemate characterised the conflict in Luhansk during these years. The Ukrainian armed forces, out of necessity and with the support of a number of Western partners, rapidly rebuilt itself into a formidable military that could draw upon a much larger economic and population base.

Even despite supply and support from Russia, the LPR and DPR could not hope to

match this rebuilt Ukrainian military. However, they had an implicit 'security guarantee' in the form of Russian military units of the Southern Military District a short distance across the border. The

An LPR militant carrying an AK-74 stands near a BMP-1 infantry fighting vehicle in a village not far from Luhansk on 12 March 2015. The BMP is probably a BMP-1P as it has a 9K113 Konkurs launcher mounted on the turret. Fitted on a special mount, the 9K113 launcher meant the BMP-1P was capable of firing the 9M113 Konkurs SACLOS anti-tank guided missile. The BMP is painted in a temporary and improvised winter camouflage scheme, common for LPR AFVs during the long winter months in Donbas. (Associated Press/Alamy Stock Photo)

Civilians crossing the partially repaired Stanytsia Luhanska bridge on foot, 2 December 2019. The flags of the LPR can be seen flying above the bridge structure. The camera looks north towards the government-controlled side of the river. (dpa picture alliance/Alamy Stock Photo)

role of the LPR armed formations was then primarily a defensive one: to fend off any sudden Ukrainian attempt to retake Luhansk oblast by force, for as long it took for massive Russian military reinforcements to arrive.

The length of the contact line in Luhansk oblast was around 170km. Starting at the east on the Russia-Ukraine border, the contact line was delineated by the Siverskyi Donets River. Moving westwards, the contact line passed between Ukrainian-held Stanytsia Luhanska and the northern outskirts of Luhansk. Here the LPR developed a large defensive position on the southern bluffs overlooking the two bridges over the river. The positions here were extensive and formed of revetted trenches and pillboxes.

The road bridge across the river at Stanytsia Luhanska had been destroyed in 2015 during the early stages of the conflict, and as many as 6,000 civilians a day crossing the contact line at Stanytsia Luhanska, many of them elderly, were forced for many years to struggle up and down the V-shaped broken bridge sections in order to cross.[29]

The Stanytsia Luhanska bridge was the only operational crossing point in Luhansk oblast. Early on in the conflict, Ukraine stopped paying pensions in the occupied territories held by the DPR and LPR. For those pensioners still living in the DPR or LPR, the only option was to cross into government-controlled areas to collect their pension there. Many other LPR civilians needed to cross to visit family members now living on the other side of the contact line, others to seek medical care on the government side.

The infamous 'broken bridge' at Stanytsia Luhanska was the scene of much civilian suffering until it was finally repaired in 2019.[30] Crucially, it was rebuilt with a much narrower repaired central span, wide enough for a civilian-type car but not for an armoured vehicle.

The contact line continued westwards, following the Siverskyi Donets River, and passing south of Shchastia which as mentioned had been recaptured by the Ukrainian armed forces. The H21 highway bridge over the river was still standing, and a small and heavily fortified Ukrainian armed forces position guarded a tiny bridgehead on the south side of the river around the bridge. Though the bridge was still intact, owing to a lack of agreement between the two sides, civilians were never able to cross the contact line here.

Continuing along the river, the contact line passed a series of small towns on the south bank of the river, all under LPR control, including Slovianoserbsk. West of these settlements, the contact line then turned south off the river, running southwest to divide the cities of Popasna (under Ukrainian control) and Pervomaisk (controlled by the LPR). It then continued running southwest, through relatively empty countryside devoid of major settlements until reaching the north side of Debaltseve in Donetsk oblast.

During this period of highly static warfare, the LPR constructed miles of defensive trenches along the contact line, as well as fortified positions in rear areas to serve as second- or third-line defences. In quieter sections, frontline positions would be manned by only small units, who observed the contact line and warned of any impending Ukrainian offensive. Some areas, like the Popasna-Pervomaisk axis, turned into regular 'hotspots' with frequent exchanges of small arms fire and artillery across the contact line.

Another feature of the contact line was the laying of barrier minefields by both sides. The LPR was recorded to have laid numerous anti-tank minefields to protect its positions, primarily surface-laid TM-62M anti-tank mines. The banks of the Siverskyi Donets River were also heavily mined with OZM-72 bounding anti-personnel mines.

Nevertheless, the geography of the contact line in Luhansk oblast favoured the LPR in its defensive role. Roughly half of the contact line it had to cover, including the sections nearest to its capital, Luhansk, was along the Siverskyi Donets River, a formidable obstacle to cross for any mechanised unit.

Luhansk Coup (November 2017)

The LPR remained an unstable political creation. In August 2016, Plotnitsky had narrowly survived an assassination attempt. Powerful factions within the LPR vied for control over power and

Unloading ammunition crates at an LPR base, 15 October 2015. In the background, a row of T-64BV main battle tanks, devoid of markings. The cockades on the hats are of the Soviet military pattern. (Associated Press/Alamy Stock Photo)

resources, each faction backed by different benefactors within the Kremlin.[31] These tensions erupted to the surface in late 2017, when Igor Plotnitsky attempted to sack the Minister of Internal Affairs, Igor Kornet, on 20 November 2017.

The following day, 21 November 2017, armed men wearing no insignia took positions in central Luhansk, including at the Ministry for Internal Affairs headquarters.[32] Kornet claimed a Ukrainian sabotage group was trying to infiltrate the LPR. Zakharchenko, the leader of the DPR, dispatched some units to assist Kornet, including members of Chechen battalion from the Special Purpose Regiment of the DPR Ministry of Defence, and at least one BTR-80 armoured personnel carrier.[33]

On 23 November 2017, Igor Plotnitsky left in a motorcade for Russia, taking several of his entourage with him. He arrived in Moscow later in the same day, and on 24 November submitted his resignation. The former head of the LPR Ministry for State Security, Leonid Pasechnik, replaced him as leader of the LPR.

Run-up to the full-scale Russian invasion of Ukraine (February 2022)

By February 2022, tensions between Ukraine and Russia had been rapidly rising. Large Russian military formations had been building up across the border in Russia and Belarus, ostensibly for a 'training exercise.'

Nevertheless in the run-up to 22 February 2022 onslaught, the force posture of the DPR and LPR forces did not markedly change. As late as 18 February 2022, the large numbers of LPR armoured fighting vehicles stored in the large weapons cantonment areas deep in LPR-controlled territory had barely moved.

It is clear though, that this was part of a calculated deception technique, as the DPR and LPR evidently had some pre-warning of the Kremlin's plans. On 18 February 2022, Denis Pushilin, leader of the DPR, announced a general mobilisation of the population, with the LPR following suit shortly afterwards.[34]

This meant that those eligible for the draft, primarily men between the ages of 18 and 55, were suddenly forbidden to leave the two People's Republics, including eastwards into Russia.[35] Simultaneously, a powerful propaganda campaign was launched, warning the DPR and LPR populations of an impending Ukrainian offensive which aimed to retake Donbas by force. This offensive was purported to begin in early March. This fabricated threat of invasion gave the justification for mass conscription and the creation of the DPR and LPR levée en masse.

A poster on the streets of Luhansk city, c. 2021. 'Russia in our hearts' reads the text, above the name of Leonid Pasechnik, Leader of the Luhansk People's Republic. (PLPK Stock Photo)

Given the general decline in population in both the DPR and LPR after 2014, this mass conscription had a huge effect on the populations of the two unrecognised states, resulting in a very high 'per capita' rate of people mobilised. In the years following 2014, many people had fled the DPR and LPR, either west to Ukrainian controlled cities or east into Russia. This was in spite of continuous efforts by the authorities in both the DPR and LPR to prevent people from leaving.

By 21 February 2022, it was reported that young people on the streets of Donetsk were being forcibly conscripted into the armed formations of the DPR.[36] According to another report, '…very few people in Luhansk volunteered to go fight against Ukraine. As a result, the military began forcibly rounding up all the men they could … The city became deserted the minute they began grabbing everyone off the streets.'[37]

Then came the moment that many in the DPR and LPR had been waiting for for many years, when, on 21 February 2022, the Kremlin officially recognised the two entities.[38] Putin took what he called the 'long overdue'[39] step of officially recognising the DPR and LPR as independent states, rather than directly annexing them into the Russian Federation as he had done with Crimea some eight years earlier. The following day, in a press conference, Putin stated that the DPR and LPR had been recognised by Russia to their pre-2014 oblast boundaries.[40] This was another ominous warning sign, as the DPR and LPR each controlled only around a third of the territory of the two pre-2014 Ukrainian oblasts at the time.

On the evening of 21 February 2022, it was reported that huge columns of regular Russian forces had entered the DPR and LPR from the east and were heading to the contact line.[41] The opening moves of Putin's 'Special Military Operation' had begun.

The 'Special Military Operation' in Luhansk oblast (February 2022 – April 2022)

In Luhansk oblast, the armed formations of the LPR were able to make rapid territorial gains. As noted, approximately half of the contact line in Luhansk oblast had been delineated by the Siverskyi Donets River, which formed a natural barrier between the two sides.

LPR propaganda messaging on the 24 February suggested that the Ukrainian military had made several attempts to cross the Siverskyi Donets, had 'been repulsed', and in response the LPR had gone on the counter-offensive. This narrative fit in well with the overall DPR and LPR messaging which had been warning the population of an impending Ukrainian offensive for over a month.

When the LPR began its assault, it struck across the Siverskyi Donets River, thereby avoiding stronger Ukrainian fortifications built along the contact line in the western part of Luhansk oblast. Nevertheless, they still faced considerable Ukrainian fortifications and minefields on the north bank of the Siverskyi Donets. An adviser to the head of the LPR noted that such fortifications meant the LPR's armed formations would not likely have an easy time of it.[42]

At Shchastia, the Ukrainian armed forces had retained control of one of the only sizeable bridges across the river still standing, the old H21 highway bridge crossing the Siverskyi Donets, and had constructed a heavily fortified strongpoint on the south side of the bridge. On 24 February, the opening of the offensive against Shchastia was announced by a member of the LPR Ministry of Internal Affairs in a post on Telegram.[43]

Heavy LPR shelling a few days earlier had damaged the massive power station built on the northern bank of the river, leaving the citizens of Shchastia without power.[44] Later on 24 February, Ukrainian forces repulsed a direct LPR attack towards the bridge, but demolished the bridge with engineering charges on the same day to slow the LPR advance.[45]

Though the attempt to seize the bridge at Shchastia was thwarted, the LPR was able to create bridgeheads elsewhere along the river. According to reports, the first crossing of the river was some 15km to the southwest of Shchastia in the vicinity of the Ukrainian village of Lopaskyne on the north bank of the Siverskyi Donets.[46] Aided by artillery fire support from regular Russian forces, the LPR's armed formations were able to secure a bridgehead close to Lopaskyne, and

construct a pontoon bridge across the river on 24 February. Thick minefields along the northern bank of the river proved an obstacle to the LPR advance. LPR forces were able to advance here to a depth of around one and a half kilometres on the first day of the assault.

Other bridgeheads were needed to widen the LPR's offensive. At the city of Stanytsia Luhanska, further to the east and closer to the Russian border, the reconstructed road bridge and the blocked railway bridge both provided crossing points over the river. Stanytsia Luhanska was reportedly captured by the LPR almost without resistance on the first day of the offensive, 24 February.

Two days later LPR militants, including those badged as JCCC (Joint Centre for Control and Coordination) liaison officers,[47] were pictured in social media posts posing in front of administration buildings in the city, and removing Ukrainian flags and state symbols.[48] In early March 2022, the Ukrainian government opened a case of treason against the head of the Stanytsia Luhanska civil-military administration and his two deputies, for allegedly switching sides and providing support to the LPR and Russian forces.[49]

The third major crossing point was at Trokhizbenka, around 20km due west of Shchastia. Here a narrow bridge carrying a minor road still crossed the Siverskyi Donets River. Though Russian sources claimed that Trokhizbenka was captured on the 25 February, Ukrainian sources suggested that the initial LPR assault on the 24 February had been repulsed, with the LPR losing two tanks and one infantry fighting vehicle.[50] By 26 February 2022, Trokhizbenka had fallen, with the LPR's 'Prizrak' Battalion reportedly capturing one of the first examples of a Javelin anti-tank missile system to fall into the hands of the armed formations.

Despite the Ukrainian demolition of the major road bridge at Shchastia on 24 February, LPR forces had crossed the river at Lopaskyne and Trokhizbenka to the west, and were able to advance on Shchastia along that axis. By 26 February LPR armed formation units had reached Shchastia and were battling for control of the city, and on 28 February the remaining Ukrainian units retreated.[51] Videos were posted celebrating the LPR 'liberation' of Shchastia, with LPR forces crossing the Siverskyi Donets by small boat underneath the destroyed H21 road bridge, and giving a tour of former Ukrainian armed forces positions on the north bank of the river to the camera crew.[52]

The Ukrainian head of the Luhansk oblast civil-military administration warned on 27 February of an impending humanitarian catastrophe in Stanytsia Luhanska and Shchastia, with the remaining civilians unable to evacuate owing to the intense fighting.[53] According to a post he placed on social media, 80 percent of the city of Shchastia had been damaged by the shelling.

With bridgeheads across the Siverskyi Donets River now secured in a number of places, the LPR was now able to advance rapidly into the rear of the Ukrainian positions along the river, and deep into northern Luhansk oblast. Avoiding the heavily fortified large urban centres of the Lysychansk/Sievierodonetsk/Rubizhne triangle on the western side of Luhansk oblast, they advanced rapidly to the northwest, with Russian sources claiming they had reached Svatove, north of Rubizhne, by 1 March.

They were assisted in this rapid advance by Russian Federation units invading Ukraine across the border into the northern part of Luhansk oblast from the east and north, placing the remaining Ukrainian units in the area in danger of being encircled. Elements of the Ukrainian 79th Air Assault Brigade, positioned north of Stanytsia Luhanska, were in danger of being encircled between the LPR's armed formations to the west and the Russian border to the east, and withdrew to the west.

The 'official' flag and crest of the LPR para-state. The flag is shown in its simplified form: without the coat of arms. The top stripe in the flag is of light blue, differentiating it from the Russian and DPR flags. The light blue was supposedly drawn from the flag of the city of Luhansk. The coat of arms of the Luhansk People's Republic, is the one adopted in October 2014 and replacing two earlier versions. Overall, the design of the coat of arms bears strong resemblance to that of the Soviet Union, with sheaves of wheat wrapped in a banner. Above the five-pointed Soviet-style red star in the centre of the emblem is an eight-pointed white star, more associated with Eastern Orthodoxy.

A modified UAZ-3151 with four PKT 7.62mm solenoid-fired machine guns on a mount in the partially-armoured rear of the vehicle, paraded by the LPR in 2021. Designed primarily for use against ground targets, the vehicle also included a pair of smoke dischargers mounted just behind the cab on the side of the armour plate. The UAZ-3151, developed in the 1980s, was a modernised version of the original UAZ-469. (Artwork by David Bocquelet)

An MT-LB VM in use by a Don Cossack unit in the LPR, c. 2015. The MT-LB VM was a modernised version of the original MT-LB. In place of the original small conical TKB-01-1 turret mounted with a PKT 7.62mm machinegun, the MT-LB VM was equipped with an NSVT 12.7mm heavy machinegun which could be fired from inside the vehicle. The MT-LB VM was never in service with the Ukrainian armed forces. This particular unit was devoid of identification numbers, common to early LPR armed formations, and was used as a prime mover for towing an MT-12 Rapira anti-tank gun. (Artwork by David Bocquelet)

An MT-LB in service with the LPR 2nd Army Corps, late 2022. Essentially, this was a standard MT-LB armoured personnel carrier and artillery tractor, with TKB-01-1 turret, painted in dark green overall, and marked with the 'Z' applied to vehicles involved in the 'special military operation'. (Artwork by David Bocquelet)

A BMP-1 infantry fighting vehicle in service with the 3rd Company of the 1st Motorised Rifle Battalion 'Zarya' of the LPR 2nd Separate Motorised Rifle Brigade, c. 2015. The BMP-1 is marked with the word *Zarya* ('Dawn') in Russian. (Artwork by David Bocquelet)

A modernised BMP-2M in service with the 6th Separate Motorised Rifle Cossack Regiment, mid-2022. Some LPR units received modernised equipment as the 'special military operation' got underway. The BMP-2M was a modernised version of the BMP-2. In addition to the 2A42 30mm cannon, an AG-17 30mm automatic grenade launcher is mounted on top of the turret. There are two missile launchers on each side of the turret capable of firing 9M133 Kornet anti-tank missiles. (Artwork by David Bocquelet)

A T-62M main battle tank as seen in service with one of the LPR armed formations, c. June 2022. The LPR and DPR began to receive supplies of the T-62M after the start of the 'special military operation' of February 2022. In addition to the T-62M's additional armour around the turret frontal arc, this T-62M, named *Nadezhda*, has had an improvised slat armour cage built over the turret. In keeping with many LPR vehicles after February 2022, there appear to be no unit markings. (Artwork by David Bocquelet)

A 2S1 Gvozdika 122mm self-propelled howitzer, in parade colour scheme, Luhansk 2016. Vehicles paraded in the LPR displayed a St George's ribbon along the side, as well as a five-pointed Soviet-style red star. Unit markings or hull numbers were not displayed on parade. (Artwork by David Bocquelet)

A 2S1 Gvozdika 122mm self-propelled howitzer in service with the LPR 2nd Separate Motorised Rifle Brigade, c. 2016. Based on the chassis of the MT-LBu multi-purpose vehicle, the Gvozdika mounted the 122mm 2A18 howitzer capable of firing conventional, high-explosive shells over a range of 15.3km. Due to the unexpectedly heavy attrition of similar, self-propelled systems in the army of the Russian Federation during the fighting in 2022, the majority of self-propelled artillery of the LNR was eventually replaced by towed pieces. (Artwork by David Bocquelet)

A T-72B main battle tank in parade colour scheme, Luhansk 2016. At 44.5 tonnes when fully loaded, this variant represented one of the best-protected and most advanced main battle tanks operated by the LPR. Huge numbers were manufactured in the 1970s, and thus large stocks were held in reserve, enabling Moscow to donate numerous examples to the LPR. (Artwork by David Bocquelet)

The LPR possessed one example of a vehicle called the 'MOP', an experimental crossing support vehicle, based on the PTS-3 amphibious transporter chassis. This one-of-a-kind vehicle, which never entered serial production, was equipped with a small turret with a 7.62mm PKT machinegun, an excavator arm, bulldozer blade, winch, and other equipment to support amphibious crossings. In addition to parades, it was used by the LPR in the field as an engineering vehicle. During such field service it was painted in improvised camouflage schemes such as the one depicted here, c. 2015. (Artwork by David Bocquelet)

A selection of unit patches of various LPR battalions. In the LPR such patches seemed to be developed mostly at battalion level, with brigades not developing particularly prevalent symbology.
Top row from left to right: The 'Batman' Rapid Response Group; 1st Motorised Rifle Battalion 'Leshy'; First Cossack Regiment of the Don Cossack Host.
Bottom row from left to right: An early pattern of patch associated with 'Prizrak,' the text at the top reading 'Novorossiya Mechanised Brigade PRIZRAK'; 3rd Motorised Rifle Battalion 'Vityaz'; A patch of the 'Army of the South-East' battalion 'Zarya.' (Author's collection and artworks by Anderson Subtil)

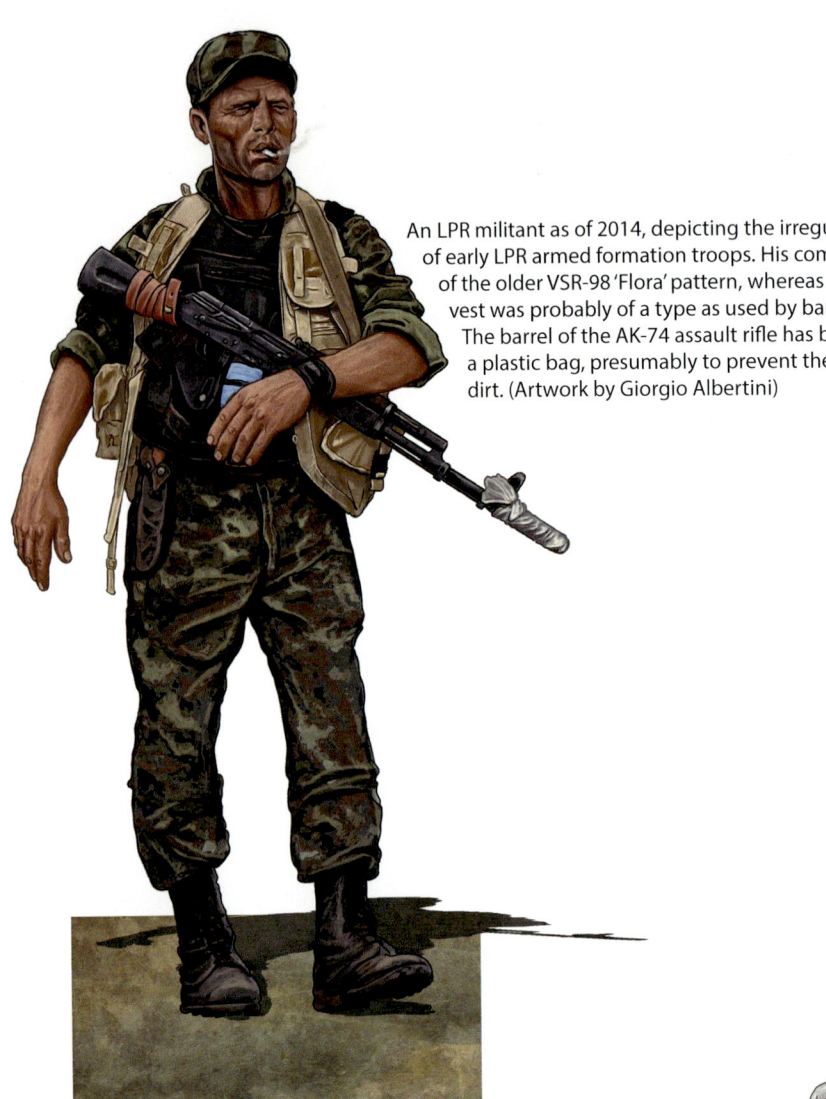

An LPR militant as of 2014, depicting the irregular appearance of early LPR armed formation troops. His combat uniform was of the older VSR-98 'Flora' pattern, whereas the black ballistic vest was probably of a type as used by bank security guards. The barrel of the AK-74 assault rifle has been covered with a plastic bag, presumably to prevent the ingress of dust or dirt. (Artwork by Giorgio Albertini)

A militant of the LPR in winter camouflage, as seen in 2015. He is shown wearing the *klyaksa* (ink blotch) camouflage pattern overall over his combat uniform, and as armed with a PKM machine gun. (Artwork by Giorgio Albertini)

A militant with the LPR Separate Commandant's Regiment, as of around 2017. On his arm is the large black brassard bearing the patch of the regiment, comprising a yellow letter 'K' on red background. Above the unit patch is the LPR flag and he is shown armed with an AKM 7.62mm assault rifle, which in the LPR seemed to be reserved for units undertaking non-frontline duties. The combat uniform and assault vest were of the standard 2008 Russian EMR 'digital flora' pattern. The white tape on his left arm was a feature of the conflict in Donbas, where units on both sides would often use different coloured tapes, displayed on uniforms and weapons, for easier identification. (Artwork by Giorgio Albertini)

An LPR militant in early 2022, wearing a combat uniform in 2008 Russian EMR 'digital flora' pattern, common to LPR armed formations after the standardisation of 2015 and 2016. He is shown armed with an AK-74 5.45mm assault rifle also standard to LPR units. (Artwork by Giorgio Albertini)

This image displays a rear car sticker at the top and two stickers below which were used to cover up the Ukrainian trident symbol bearing the letters UA on car number plates when the conflict started in 2014. As time progressed the stickers were no longer needed as new metal number plates had the Ukrainian symbols removed and they were replaced with that of the LPR and its own tricolour flag. (Dean O'Brien collection)

A collection of fridge magnets and a keyring displaying the coat of arms of the Lugansk People's Republic. (Dean O'Brien collection)

A car pennant displaying the coat of arms of the Lugansk People's Republic. (Dean O'Brien collection)

A bust of Lenin sits proudly in front of three table flags on an office desk. This is a common sight in almost every office in the Donetsk and Lugansk People's Republics. (Dean O'Brien collection)

Since 2014 and Luhansk claiming its independence, there have been numerous variations of their flag. This is just a small sample of the versions that have been created since 2014.

Another variation of the Luhansk flag.

In this flag a Russian soldier stands in front of both the Donbass and Lugansk People's Republics flags with the message 'Donbass Will Not Surrender'.

This flag features the Russian Imperial flag which displays the words 'We are Russian God is With Us'.

This is the flag of 'Novorossiya' (new Russia) which features the crest of arms bearing the words 'Novorossiya – Will and Work'.

Another flag of 'Novorossiya' (new Russia) but without the crest. Both versions have been in use since 2014 and are still seen on the battlefield today.

This flag is known as the Gonfalon/Mandylion. It depicts the face of Christ and it originates from the Orthodox icon 'Not Made By Hands'. These flags are often blessed by Orthodox priests and handed out to battalions heading to the front.

(All flag images from the Dean O'Brien collection)

0   25   75km

RUSSIA

Urazovo

Troitske

Roven'ki

Kantemirovka

Kivsharivka

Novopskov

Markivka

Chertkovo

Bilokurakyne

Svatove

Starobil's'k

Bilovods'k

Yevsuh

Millerovo

Lyman

Rubizhne

Sieverodonetsk

Lysychansk

Shchastia

Stanytsia
Luhanska

Kramatorsk

Glubokii

Bakhmut

Popasna

A

F

Luhansk

B   **C**

D   **E**

Lutuhyne

Donetsk

Sorokyne

K

Horlivka

Debaltseve

UKRAINE

Khrustalnyi

Antratsyt

I

Dovzhansk

G

H

Rovenky

J

Gukovo

Snizhne

Donetsk

Ilovais'k

Kuibysnevo

Shakhty

Major urban areas (former names in brackets):

A Holubivka
(Kirovsk)

D Kadiivka
(Stakhanov)

G Khrustalnyi
(Krasnyi Luch)

J Dovzhansk
(Sverdlovsk)

B Pervomaisk

E Alchevsk

H Antratsyt

K Sorokyne
(Krasnodon)

C Brianka

F Luhansk

I Rovenky

Map by Paul Hewitt

Ukrainian units began to pull back towards Sievierodonetsk/ Lysychansk/Rubizhne, all large cities in the western part of Luhansk oblast and comprising the 'triangle' of industrial cities which had been freed from LPR control during the Ukrainian ATO in 2014. During these days of rapid territorial gains, the LPR was publishing a daily list of towns 'liberated' from Ukrainian control.

On 28 February, a heavily fortified second-line Ukrainian position some 6km north of Stanytsia Luhanska in the suburb of Makarove, was reportedly captured by the LPR with minimal resistance, after Ukrainian units withdrew.[54] The capture of this extensive strongpoint, constructed over eight years of static conflict on some commanding heights overlooking the P22 highway, was a major propaganda victory for the LPR.

On 3 March, LPR armed formations and Russian Federation forces met in Novoaidar, 30km northwest of Shchastia, in a highly-publicised symbolic event. In an event likely choreographed for the Russian TV cameras, LPR forces approaching from the south encountered Russian forces advancing from the north.[55] Russian journalists present commented on the difference between the regular Russian and irregular LPR forces, noting the differences between the old BMPs and MT-LBs of the LPR in 'motley camouflage' and the modern BMP-3s of the Russian forces.[56] In fact, the first actual meeting of such forces was likely to have taken place at least two days earlier, and further to the northwest.

On Saturday 5 March, LPR armed formations swinging around the northern side of the Sievierodonetsk/Lysychansk/Rubizhne urban conurbation were now entering the northeastern part of Donetsk oblast, reportedly capturing small towns and villages around 20km northeast of the city of Sloviansk.

On 22 March 2022, the head of the LPR, Leonid Pasechnik, said that around 80 percent of Luhansk oblast was then under the control of the LPR, with the major cities of Popasna, Rubizhne, Lysychansk, Sievierodonetsk and Kreminna still under Ukrainian control.[57] He also stated that in areas that had been taken by the LPR, the pattern of life for civilians was being normalised, with agricultural businesses working again, and pension payments being made in Stanytsia Luhanska 'on a trial basis.'[58]

However, much of the territory captured by the LPR and Russian forces on the north side of the Siverskyi Donets River was agricultural land dotted with small villages or towns. The remaining cities under Ukrainian control in Luhansk oblast, in particular the Sievierodonetsk/Lysychansk/Rubizhne triangle and Popasna, were all sizeable cities which the defending Ukrainian forces had had time to fortify. They would be much harder to capture, and Russia had not deployed sufficient combat units in Donbas to undertake the task.

For their part, the LPR armed formations, having already suffered heavy casualties, were also utilising fresh conscripts generated by the mass mobilisation of mid-February 2022, many of whom had not received adequate training or equipment. In many places they were also being thrown into frontal assaults against prepared Ukrainian defences. One Russian volunteer, considering whether to join the D/LPR armed formations in 2022 '…finally decided that "whether due to stupidity or intentionally, Moscow is ruining the Donbas infantry by sending them into senseless and disorganized attacks. I don't want to go there."'[59]

Reports flowed in of the new recruits in the LPR's armed formations facing 'a lack of medical care, military gear, and even food.'[60] According to the Eastern Human Rights Group,

Local residents line up to receive humanitarian aid next to an exhibition of captured Ukrainian tanks and weapons in Lysychansk, 12 July 2022. A school building in the background has been all but destroyed in the fighting. An LPR militant at the bottom left of the picture wears a brassard bearing the red patch of the LPR Separate Commandant's Regiment. On each side of the static displays of weaponry put on for journalists, banners in the colours of the LPR flag have been displayed on stands. (Associated Press/Alamy Stock Photo)

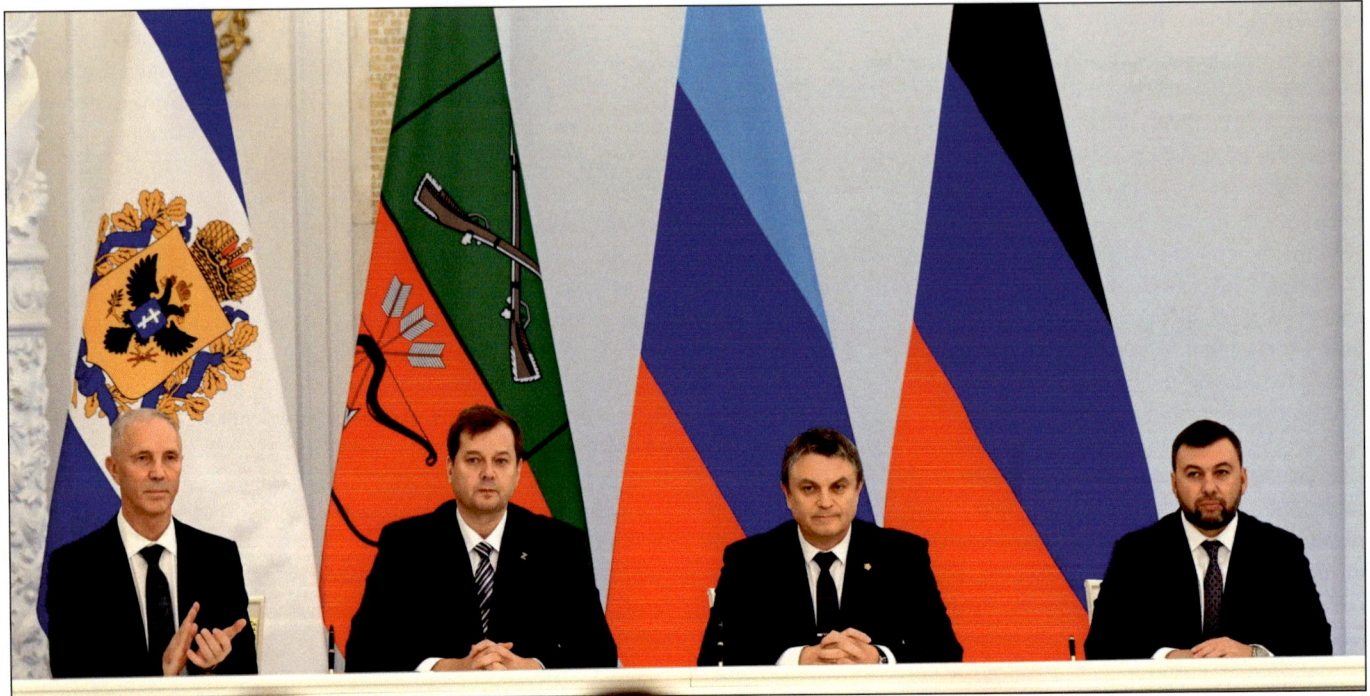

From left, Moscow-appointed head of Kherson region Vladimir Saldo, Moscow-appointed head of Zaporizhzhia region Yevgeny Balitsky, Leonid Pasechnik, leader of the LPR, and Denis Pushilin, leader of the DPR attend a ceremony to sign the treaties for four regions of Ukraine to join Russia, at the Kremlin on 30 September 2022. The signing of the treaties making the four regions part of Russia followed the completion of the Kremlin-orchestrated referendums in those regions. (Associated Press/Alamy Stock Photo)

approximately 140,000 people had been mobilised by the two People's Republics by June 2022.[61]

Pictures and videos emerged of whole units of mobilised recruits in the LPR's 2nd Army Corps carrying 7.62mm Mosin–Nagant bolt action rifles. Documents captured by Ukrainian forces after the Kharkiv counter-offensive revealed small details such as an injury to one LPR militant from a Mosin–Nagant chamber explosion, and also the age of one mobilisee from the LPR, a corporal 64 years of age.[62]

Renewed Russian offensive in the Donbas (April 2022 – June 2022)

In the wake of Russia's failed attempt to capture Kyiv and effectively deal a coup de grace to the Ukrainian government, Russia withdrew its forces from the Kyiv region and redeployed to focus on eastern and southern Ukraine. This meant that Russian and LPR forces now had sufficient combat power to attempt to capture the major cities in Luhansk oblast still under Ukrainian control.

After this failure to win a rapid and decisive victory in Kyiv by utilising light airborne forces and a lightning dash to the Ukrainian capital, the Russian forces in Donbas, backed by their DPR and LPR proxies, reverted to a different style of warfare comprising a slow grinding offensive preceded by heavy artillery bombardment.

By 18 April 2022 it had concentrated its units along the contact line in eastern Ukraine, and began a new large-scale offensive, opening with an intense artillery barrage. Kreminna fell on the same day, reported by the Ukrainian head of the Luhansk regional military administration, Serhii Haidai.[63] In the battle for Kreminna, an LPR commander of one of the Cossack battalions was killed.[64] The capture of Kreminna meant that Sievierodonetsk/Lysychansk/Rubizhne were in increasing danger of encirclement by LPR/Russian forces. Civilian casualties mounted, as Russian artillery pounded these cities.

Capture of Luhansk oblast and annexation by Russia (June 2022 – September 2022)

On 7 May, LPR and Russian forces captured Popasna, and from there were able to begin an attempt to encircle Sievierodonetsk from the south, as well as from Kreminna in the north. Nevertheless, Ukrainian forces in Sievierodonetsk held out for many weeks, the city finally falling on 24 June after one of the bloodiest and most destructive battles in Donbas.

Ukrainian forces then mounted a stiff defence of Lysychansk to the west, which was considered a more defensible city, and one where Ukrainian units occupied the high ground overlooking the Siverskyi Donets River. After heavy fighting, and a heavy bombardment by Russian artillery and airpower, Lysychansk too was captured by the LPR and Russian forces on 3 July 2022. As at Sievierodonetsk, massive destruction had been wreaked on the city and its inhabitants.

With the capture of Lysychansk, the LPR was now in control of effectively all of Luhansk oblast. Russian cosmonauts on the International Space Station posed with an LPR flag and an accompanying Tweet proclaimed 3 July 2022 as a new 'Great Victory Day' in reference to the 9 May celebration commemorating the Soviet victory during the Second World War.[65] Putin praised the capture of Lysychansk and stated that Russian and LPR forces there would pause to allow them to rebuild their combat capabilities.[66]

The LPR would retain control over all of Luhansk oblast until 4 September 2022, when the village of Bilhorivka on the border with Donetsk oblast was recaptured by Ukrainian forces as part of the Kharkiv offensive.

From 23 to 27 September 2022, the LPR held a referendum on joining Russia, joining parts of three other regions occupied by Russian forces in Donetsk, Kherson and Zaporizhzhia oblasts. The vote was condemned as an illegal 'sham' by Ukraine, and there were reports of people being forced to vote. In the town of Starobilsk in Luhansk oblast, residents were prevented from leaving while voting was taking place, and people were coerced from their homes in order to take part.[67]

After the referendum achieved an almost unanimous positive result, on 30 September 2022, the LPR was formally annexed by Russia, and ceased to exist as a nominally independent identity. The 'Crimean scenario' so long awaited by many LPR militants, had finally occurred.

6

COMMAND AND CONTROL OF LPR 2ND ARMY CORPS

As the early, disorganised and almost leaderless early formations of the LPR began to coalesce into larger formations and ultimately into the LPR 2nd Army Corps, they came to rely more and more on military, logistical and political support from the Russian Federation. In Moscow, so-called 'curators' advised on and pushed LPR and DPR agendas within the Kremlin.

At a military level, some Ukrainian sources claimed that the DPR 1st Army Corps and LPR 2nd Army Corps were directly controlled as subordinate units within the 8th Army of the Russian Federation's Southern Military District.[1] Other analysts agreed with this 'direct control' theory, positing that: 'The rebel armed forces in eastern Ukraine are regarded as reserve formations of the Russian armed forces (probably at the formal rank of auxiliary territorial defence troops in order to differentiate them from regular Russian troops).'[2]

This theory held that the vast majority of staff officer and command positions within the LPR and DPR armed formations were occupied by up to 2,000 senior officers from the Russian armed forces, who were posted on a rotational basis, while the lower ranks were filled with 'Donbas locals.'[3]

Many Western observers of the conflict in Donbas shared this view, emphasising the importance of the Southern Military District to Russian military planning, and the ways in which the Southern Military District provided support to the armed formations of the DPR and LPR.[4]

The idea that the armed formations of the LPR and DPR were a formal extension of Russian forces also suited the Ukrainian narrative from 2014 to 2022 which sought to frame the conflict as an international one, downplaying any indigenous dimensions to the conflict. In this way the LPR armed formations (as well as those of the neighbouring DPR) were commonly described by the Ukrainian government and military as the 'occupying forces of the Russian Federation in the Donbas' (in Ukrainian: Окупаційні війська РФ на Донбасі).

As Ukraine struggled for more Western support for the conflict in Donbas, it understandably sought to place blame for the conflict on Russia as an aggressor country. Ukraine steadfastly refused to directly negotiate with representatives from the DPR and LPR, labelling them as criminals or terrorists. The Ukrainian government also feared that negotiating with them would be seen as giving them legitimacy.

This central tenet of Ukrainian policy was enshrined in the legal system, including the 2018 law 'On the state policy to ensure the state sovereignty of Ukraine in the temporarily occupied territories in Donetsk and Luhansk regions.' This law firmly framed Russia as the aggressor country, temporarily occupying the Donetsk and Luhansk NGCAs, and therefore precluded any ceding of 'authority' by Ukraine to the DPR and LPR.[5]

Failure of the Novorossiya Confederation Project

However, irrespective of the outside perception of the LPR 2nd Army Corps as a formal extension of Russian Southern Military District, it is evident that the units of the LPR 2nd Army Corps, and indeed the LPR as an entity more broadly, had an autonomy that it frequently exercised. Simply put, Russian control of the DPR and LPR had its limits. The Russian Foreign Minister Sergei Lavrov grudgingly '… acknowledged Moscow's influence with the separatists, but he also insisted that it was not "as great as 100 percent."'[6]

Furthermore, in LPR there was little appetite for confederation with the DPR into the much-anticipated political entity of 'Novorossiya' touted by Dugin and other pro-Russian Eurasianists. One of the early DPR leaders, Alexander Borodai, gave his opinion on the lack of union between the two Republics, stating that the '…Lugansk elite was apprehensive of the Donetsk one which was richer, more numerous and more charismatic. As a result, the idea of unification was immediately rejected on the Lugansk initiative out of the fear that they will be overpowered by Donetsk.'[7]

This early and publicly announced failure of the 'Novorossiya Project' exposed the differences between the de facto authorities of the two regions. Announced in May 2014 as a confederation of the two areas, and referenced by Putin in his speeches, less than a year later it was announced that the political project would be cancelled, and the DPR and LPR would remain as two distinct entities. As a result, the initial plan to create a joint military structure covering the two areas, the United Armed Forces of Novorossiya, was also dropped.

This failure to merge the DPR and LPR into a single political structure led to the concomitant creation of two army corps to match these two entities,[8] the 1st Army Corps for the DPR and the 2nd Army Corps for the LPR.

This casts a different light on the 'total control' that many Western analysts supposed that Russia wielded over the LPR and DPR. In fact it suggests the contrary, and that the '…objectives of the separatist movement in Donbas very quickly came to be at odds with the Kremlin's. As a result, the Donetsk and Lugansk People's Republics … proved highly ineffective proxies for Moscow, which realized, over the course of 2014 and 2015, that its control over them was limited.'[9]

7
LPR 2ND ARMY CORPS AND PRINCIPAL UNITS

The LPR's 2nd Army Corps was officially formed on 7 October 2014, unit number 77077, headquartered in Luhansk. This section will provide an overview of the principle LPR 2nd Army Corps units after the Corp's creation in 2014. It aims to describe the structure of the LPR 2nd Army Corps between 2016 and early 2022, during which time the structure was fairly stable. The creation of new LPR regiments after February 2022, about which relatively little is known at the time of writing, will also be discussed.

There is some debate about whether, around 2016, the LPR 2nd Army Corps was renamed the 'Operational-Tactical Command "Luhansk" of the LPR Ministry of Defence.'[1] However, such changes in terminology do not alter the fact that the LPR 2nd Army Corps existed within the area controlled by the LPR, and had a fairly well-defined structure that remained fairly stable from early 2016 to early 2022. For this reason, the book will refer to LPR 2nd Army Corps as the overall umbrella unit for the vast majority of the LPR's frontline military strength, despite possible minor changes to its nomenclature.

The LPR 2nd Army Corps was smaller than the DPR 1st Army Corps, fielding only four combat brigades, one of which (the 7th) was effectively a DPR armed formation which had been subordinated to the 2nd Army Corps. Like the 1st Army Corps, the LPR 2nd Army Corps was broadly defensive in its composition, it was noted that it only possessed motorised rifle brigades and an artillery brigade, there was no tank brigade to give it greater offensive capability.[2]

A notable feature of brigades in the LPR 2nd Army Corps is that they were not usually named, with the exception of the 7th 'Chistyakov' Brigade, which as noted was transferred from the DPR 1st Army Corps. In addition, there was not a particularly strong unit symbology at brigade level in the LPR, with unit symbology and patches being prevalent only at battalion level – a reflection perhaps of the fragmented manner in which the LPR 2nd Army Corps units came together.

In 2016, Ukrainian estimates put the total strength of DPR 1st Army Corps at 20,000 people, compared to just under 15,000 for the LPR 2nd Army Corps.[3] However, Ukrainian sources suggested that while most DPR brigades were undermanned, the brigades of the LPR 2nd Army Corps had more combat power than equivalent DPR brigades owing to more complete staffing levels.[4] By 2019, the LPR 2nd Army Corps was estimated to comprise 14,727 personnel, 196 tanks, 357 armoured fighting vehicles, 204 artillery pieces, 86 MLRS, and 105 mortars.[5]

Major weapons storage areas

The LPR 2nd Army Corps developed huge weapons storage areas where it stored and maintained heavy military equipment including main battle tanks, infantry fighting vehicles, artillery and armoured personnel carriers.

These extensive bases could be seen on open-source satellite imagery/mapping websites, and comprised rows of vehicle stands, usually protected with individual revetments. Several such sites were even denoted with pins on Google Maps as 'Сепарська база техніки' ('Separatist military equipment base' in Ukrainian). The three largest bases were located at Myrne, Buhaivka near Perevalsk, and Shymshynivka, all in the general area between the cities of

LPR 2nd Army Corps subdued patch, c. 2016. In the absence of a strong brigade-level symbology, this LPR 2nd Army Corps patch was perhaps the one most commonly seen on LPR militants after 2015, aside from the Novorossiya flag. (Private collection, used with permission)

Alchevsk and Luhansk. These sites each contained hundreds of revetments.

Another site where LPR military equipment was displayed was at 'Patriot Park' situated on the main runway of the old Luhansk International Airport. Opened in 2019 by Leonid Pasechnik, the park contained a row of military equipment types used by the LPR, one of each type.[6] The name of the park evidently mimicked that of the military-patriotic park near Moscow, which opened in 2016. Items of equipment stored at the museum were painted in an unusual green/yellow/brown camouflage scheme, and were marked with St George's black and orange stripes. In 2022 all the vehicles present vanished from satellite imagery, possibly returned to active service.

Tactical symbols

Like in the DPR, early LPR armed formation units had a diverse set of tactical symbols, comprising triangles, rhomboids or diamonds with numbers or symbols inside. The LPR 2nd brigade, for example, had an early symbol depicting a circle inside an equilateral triangle. Vehicles used by 'Prizrak' displayed a white diamond with a Russian letter 'P' inside.

By late 2018, the LPR 2nd Army Corps had settled on squares to denote all units, whether brigade, battalion or company level. Numbers inside these shapes denoted the actual unit. This was in contrast to the DPR, which by then used triangles for brigades, squares for regiments, and circles for battalions.

In terms of the overall numbering system, in general brigades belonging to the DPR 1st Army Corps were generally assigned odd numbers, and those belonging to the LPR 2nd Army Corps were allocated even numbers.[7]

A 2S1 Gvozdika 122mm self-propelled howitzer displayed at Patriot Park in Luhansk, on the main runway of the former Luhansk International Airport, 23 February 2020. (Global Look Press/Alamy Stock Photo)

2nd Separate Motorised Rifle Brigade (2-я Отдельная Мотострелковая Бригада)

The LPR 2nd Separate Motorised Rifle Brigade was the most powerful armed formation in the LPR. It was formed of three early LPR battalions, which were formed into the 2nd Brigade on 1 November 2014.[8] These battalions 'Zarya', which became the 1st Motorised Rifle Battalion; 'Don,' which became the 2nd Motorised Rifle Battalion; and 'Hooligan,' which became the 3rd.

'Zarya' ('Dawn') was originally formed in early 2014 as the 1st LNOB (Luhansk People's Liberation Battalion/ Луганский Народно-освободительный батальон), part of the 'Army of the South-East.' 'Zarya' had been founded by Plotnitsky, and as such, remained one of the LPR's most important battalions. 'The main Luhansk battalion was *Zarya* (Dawn) commanded by Igor Plotnitsky, later the LNR premier […] Zarya's core was made up of the former security

personnel with an anti-Maidan orientation and "Afghantsy," who were joined by local Luhansk men of all kinds of social origins.'[9]

These three battalions were then supplemented by a tank battalion equipped with T-64BV main battle tanks, a self-propelled artillery

A T-64BV main battle tank in a defensive position, north of Luhansk city on 14 January 2015. On the vehicle searchlight is a circle within a triangle, an early tactical symbol of the LPR 2nd Motorised Rifle Brigade. (Mstyslav Chernov/Associated Press/Alamy Stock Photo)

Key units of the LPR 2nd Army Corps (2014-2022)				
Type of unit	**Name of unit**	**Unit number and unit tactical sign displayed in a square [X]**	**HQ (if known)**	**Composition/notable units**
Brigade	2nd Separate Motorised Rifle Brigade	73438 [2]	Luhansk	1st Motorised Rifle Battalion 'Zarya'
				2nd Motorised Rifle Battalion 'Don'
				3rd Motorised Rifle Battalion 'Hooligan'
				Tank battalion
				Self-propelled artillery battalion
				Towed artillery battalion
				Rocket artillery battalion
	4th Separate Motorised Rifle Brigade	74347 [4]	Alchevsk	1st Motorised Rifle Battalion 'Leshy'
				2nd Motorised Rifle Battalion 'Batman'
				3rd Motorised Rifle Battalion 'Vityaz'
				14th Separate Special Battalion 'Prizrak'
				Tank battalion
				Self-propelled artillery battalion
				Towed artillery battalion
				Rocket artillery battalion
	7th Separate Guards Motorised Rifle 'Chistyakov' Brigade	08807 [7]	Debaltseve	1st Motorised Rifle Battalion
				2nd Motorised Rifle Battalion
				3rd Motorised Rifle Battalion
				Tank battalion
				Self-propelled artillery battalion
				Towed artillery battalion
				Rocket artillery battalion
	10th Separate Artillery Brigade	23213 [10]	Khrustalni/ Luhansk	Reconnaissance battalion
				1st artillery battalion
				2nd artillery battalion
				Anti-tank divizion
				Howitzer artillery battalion
				Self-propelled artillery battalion
Regiment	6th Separate Motorised Rifle Cossack Regiment named after Matvey Platov	69647 [6]	Kadiivka	
	Separate Commandant's Regiment	44444 [22]	Luhansk	1st Battalion
				2nd Battalion
				Guard Company
Battalion	4th Separate Tank Battalion	64064 [8]	Luhansk	1st tank company
				2nd tank company
				3rd tank company
				4th tank company
				Motorised rifle company
				Artillery divizion

battalion equipped with 2S1 Gvozdika 122mm self-propelled howitzers, a rocket artillery battalion equipped with BM-21 Grad 122mm MLRS, and a howitzer artillery battalion equipped with D-30 12mm towed artillery pieces.

In 2014, a unit symbol of a circle in a triangle was seen on 2nd Motorised Rifle Brigade vehicles and equipment, this was later replaced by the standardised LPR marking of a number '2' in a square.

By mid-2015, the strength of the LPR 2nd Motorised Rifle Brigade was thought to be around 4,500 personnel. Ukrainian analysts considered the LPR 2nd Motorised Rifle Brigade to be one of the most powerful units in the DPR and LPR, partly owing to the fact that it consistently had the highest staffing level compared to other units.

In 2016, the leader of the LPR at the time, Igor Plotnitsky, named the brigade after the Hero of the Soviet Union Marshal Kliment Voroshilov.[10] In addition to the honorary 'Guards' designation the brigade had already acquired, its full official name then became the '2nd Separate Guards Motorised Rifle Brigade named after the Hero of the Soviet Union Kliment Efremovich Voroshilov of the People's Militia of the Lugansk People's Republic' (Вторая отдельная гвардейская мотострелковая бригада имени Героя Советского Союза Климента Ефремовича Ворошилова Народной милиции Луганской Народной Республики).

4th Separate Motorised Rifle Brigade (4-я Отдельная Мотострелковая Бригада)

Based in Alchevsk, the 4th Separate Motorised Rifle Brigade eventually absorbed a number of the LPR's most famous independent battalions from the start of the conflict in Donbas, in particular 'Batman' and 'Prizrak.'

The 1st Motorised Rifle Battalion 'Leshy' («Леший», 'Troll' in English) was formed during the violent protests in Luhansk across April 2014. At first numbering no more than 20 or 30 individuals,

the group, led by an Alexei Pavlov, seized the Security Service of Ukraine (SBU) building in Luhansk on 6 April 2014. The battalion's original core members were mostly from the city of Kadiivka (formerly Stakhanov), and later the battalion was referred to as a Special Forces Battalion. By September 2014, it numbered around 800 militants.[11]

The 2nd Motorised Rifle Battalion 'Batman' («Бэтмен») derived from one of the highest profile LPR battalions which traced its origins to early 2014, commanded by Oleksander Bednov. A former riot policeman, Bednov formed the 'Batman' Rapid Response Group (Группа быстрого реагирования) in April 2014, at first it numbered only 12 men armed with only a few machine guns.[12] The battalion's name was derived from Bednov's own nom-de-guerre.

Bednov was instrumental in helping to build the unified LPR 2nd Army Corps, by bringing together the disparate battalions. When 'Batman' was brought into the 4th Separate Motorised Rifle Brigade, he went on to serve as the Brigade's Chief of Staff.[13] He reportedly disagreed with the LPR leadership on the signing of the Minsk agreements, and advocated for the continuation of hostilities until all of Luhansk oblast was under LPR control. Bednov was subsequently killed in an ambush on 1 January 2015, the weapon used was supposedly an RPO-A Shmel single-shot rocket launched thermobaric weapon.

Also in the 4th Separate Motorised Rifle Brigade was the 3rd Motor Rifle Battalion 'Vityaz.' This unit maintained a very low profile online, and remained one of the more mysterious units within the LPR. There is compelling evidence to suggest that 'Vityaz' was comprised primarily of Russian soldiers from the 15th Separate Motorised Rifle 'Peacekeeping' Brigade from the Russian Federation's Central Military District (unit number 90600).[14]

Similarly, other analysis suggested that battalion tactical groups of the 15th Separate Motorised Rifle 'Peacekeeping' Brigade had been used on a 'raid and withdraw' principle in Donbas in order to assist DPR and LPR forces,[15] and thereby that this 're-badging' of

An LPR improvised technical being driven in a parade in Luhansk city, 14 September 2014. Mounted on the back underneath an improvised gun shield is an NSV 12.7mm machine gun. The LPR militant holding the NSV wears the 'bat symbol' patch of the 'Batman' Rapid Response Group, the symbol of which is also spraypainted on the vehicle door. A Russian flag and that of Novorossiya are prominently displayed. (Associated Press / Alamy Stock Photo)

Alexei Mozgovoi, leader of 'Prizrak' battalion, photographed on 8 November 2014. (Associated Press/Alamy Stock Photo)

'Peacekeeping' units as the 3rd Motor Rifle Battalion 'Vityaz' was a continuation of this trend.

This is a hand embroidered piece of artwork bearing the image of Aleksey Mozgovoy and was given to a journalist working in the Donbass region. (Dean O'Brien collection)

Another notable battalion brought into the 4th Separate Motorised Rifle Brigade was 'Prizrak' («Призрак», which means 'Ghost' in English). The name was apparently a defiant reference to the repeated reported demise of the unit in the Ukrainian media. 'Prizrak' was founded by one of the LPR's best known military commanders, Alexei Mozgovoi, in April 2014 as a 'self-defence unit.'

LPR militants stand guard during the funeral of prominent commander Alexei Mozgovoi in Alchevsk, 27 May 2015. Alexei Mozgovoi and at least six other people were killed when his vehicle was ripped apart by a bomb and then strafed by gunfire. The individual on the left holds an AK-74 5.45mm assault rifle and wears a St. George's ribbon. The fighter closest to the camera wears a Gorka 3 suit. As well as being used in the current conflict since 2014, the Gorka suit was previously worn by fighters in both the Afghan and Chechen wars. On the left breast he wears a Soviet Guards badge which dates back to May 1942 when they were first introduced. The images to the right show details of this style of badge which, rather than having a pin fixing on the rear, are secured using a threaded screw back. (Associated Press/Alamy Stock Photo and Dean O'Brien collection)

The battalion, '…which operated outside of the LNR command occupied a special space in the rebellion history both inspirationally and as a combat force. It was set up in Stakhanov and later based in Alchevsk. *Prizrak* was headed by Alexei Mozgovoi […] Mozgovoi in his civilian incarnation was a local singer and used to perform in a club in Svatove.'[16]

Despite being a unit operational primarily in Luhansk oblast in 2014, 'Prizrak' worked closely with Igor 'Strelkov' Girkin (a key early DPR military commander), reportedly coordinating their actions with him. 'Prizrak' was thus '…was the only force in the "LPR" to cooperate with Igor Girkin/Strelkov's forces in the Donetsk "people's republic"'[17].

Furthermore, '…Mozgovoi established contacts with Vladimir Zhirinovsky, the leader of the Liberal-Democratic Party of Russia (LDPR), and his camp was filled with LDPR T-shirts and other memorabilia.'[18] Zhirinovsky also donated an armoured GAZ Tigr, which was painted bright blue and was driven around by LPR militants until it was crashed in September 2014.[19]

'Prizrak' fought Ukrainian units in the city of Lysychansk until being ordered to withdraw in late July 2014, moving south to the industrial city of Alchevsk. However, fighting the mechanised units of the Ukrainian ATO evidently took a heavy toll on the original 'core' of the battalion. Interviewing militants who served in 'Prizrak,' Matveeva wrote that: 'One rebel who fought with it

Members of 'Prizrak' ride atop a BTR-80 armoured personnel carrier at the head of a funeral procession for prominent commander Alexei Mozgovoi in Alchevsk, 27 May 2015. The BTR-80 is marked with a Russian letter 'P' in a diamond, as well as the 'Prizrak' ghost insignia. (Mstyslav Chernov/Associated Press/Alamy Stock Photo)

Two boys watch as an LPR convoy rolls along the streets of Kadiivka (formerly Stakhanov) in Luhansk oblast on 24 April 2015. The BMP-1 infantry fighting vehicle is marked with a '4' in a white square, denoting it as belonging to the LPR 4th Separate Motorised Rifle Brigade. It is painted in an unusual brown and green camouflage pattern. (Associated Press/Alamy Stock Photo)

expressed his disappointment saying to me that "*Prizrak* perished under the tanks at Lysychansk, it was all downhill after that."'[20]

By August 2014 Mozgovoi was referring to the unit as a 'brigade' and stated that the unit numbered 1,000 people, including volunteers from Russia, Bulgaria, Slovakia and Germany.[21] In March 2015, part of 'Prizrak' was redesignated as the 4th Territorial Defence Battalion of the LPR, part of the wider reorganisation of LPR forces into the 2nd Army Corps.

Like Oleksander Bednov, Mozgovoi was a fierce critic of the Minsk accords and the LPR leadership. He was also a very popular military commander who – like commanders such as 'Givi' and 'Motorola' in Donetsk – was developing an almost cult-like following of his own, challenging the authority of senior LPR figures.

On 23 May 2015, Mozgovoi was killed in an ambush on his vehicle deep inside LPR-controlled territory. In January 2016, the remainder of 'Prizrak' was brought into the 4th Separate Motorised Rifle Brigade, as the 14th Separate Special Battalion 'Prizrak.'

The 4th Separate Motorised Rifle Brigade had, like all LPR motorised rifle brigades, organic air defence assets in the form of 9K38 Igla MANPADS (Man-Portable Air Defence Systems), and units from the 4th Brigade were filmed firing such MANPADS during a training exercise in 2017.[22]

In May 2023, the commander of the 4th Separate Motorised Rifle Brigade was killed in fighting near Bakhmut, in Donetsk oblast.[23] After the start of Putin's 'special military operation' the LPR 2nd Army Corps was deployed outside the boundaries of Luhansk oblast as the Russian advance bore down on Ukrainian cities such as Kharkiv and Bakhmut.

7th Separate Guards Motorised Rifle 'Chistyakov' Brigade (7-я отдельная гвардейская мотострелковая Чистяковская бригада)

The 7th Separate Guards Motorised Rifle 'Chistyakov' Brigade was formed in Torez, in Donetsk oblast, from part of the group of militants who had fought under Igor 'Strelkov' Girkin in Sloviansk and escaped from encirclement there.

For a short period of time in 2015, part of Girkin's 'Slavyansk' Brigade was formed into the DPR 1st Army Corps 7th Slavyansk Motorised Rifle Brigade (unit number 08807).[24] This brigade had at least one motorised rifle battalion. At an unknown date in late 2015, the 7th Slavyansk Motorised Rifle Brigade was transferred to the LPR 2nd Army Corps, and disappeared from the DPR 1st Army Corps order of battle.

As such, 'Chistyakov' retained a number of DPR-like features. Firstly, it was allocated an odd brigade number as opposed to the even numbers usually given to LPR brigades. Secondly, the fact it was a named brigade, 'Chistyakov.' The name was given to the brigade after the capture of Debaltseve by combined DPR, LPR and Russian forces, taking the name of a Soviet-era formation which took part in operations in Donbas during the Second World War. Thirdly, it had geographic responsibility for part of the contact line from 2015 to 2022 which included Debaltseve in Donetsk oblast.

The strategically important transport hub of Debaltseve was geographically situated within the boundaries of Donetsk oblast, and fell under the control of the DPR in terms of civilian administration. The LPR 7th Brigade was also positioned in several smaller towns and villages to the west of Debaltseve, where its area of responsibility abutted that of the DPR 3rd Separate Motorised Rifle Brigade 'Berkut.'

In general structure, the 7th Brigade followed the usual pattern for LPR brigades, with three motorised rifle battalions, a tank battalion, a self-propelled artillery battalion equipped with 2S1 Gvozdika self-propelled howitzers, a towed artillery battalion, a rocket artillery battalion equipped with BM-21 Grad MLRS, and an anti-aircraft missile *divizion*.[25] In October 2018, the brigade was awarded the honorary title of 'Guards' by the head of the LPR, Leonid Pasechnik.[26]

Unit marking was initially a Roman numeral 'VII' in a pentagon, later changed to a Latin number '7' in a diamond shape. At some point after its transfer to the LPR 2nd Army Corps, the markings painted on vehicles used by the brigade were changed to the LPR standard of a number '7' in a white square.

7th Separate Guards Motorised Rifle 'Chistyakov' Brigade subdued patch, c. 2017. At the top is the name of the brigade, 'Chistyakov,' and around the bottom a motto, loosely translated as 'Born in the fire' (Private collection, used with permission)

A BMP-1P infantry fighting vehicle belonging to the 7th Separate Motorised Rifle 'Chistyakov' Brigade, guarding the crash site of Malaysian Airlines MH17 plane near the village of Hrabove, Donetsk oblast, during a media visit on 16 July 2015. The fighters said they arrived to protect the media and made sure the MH17 crash site was cleared of ammunition and mines. The Brigade tactical symbol at the time, a '7' in a diamond, is painted on the side of the BMP. (Associated Press/Alamy Stock Photo)

10th Separate Artillery Brigade (10-я отдельная артиллерийская бригада)

The last of the LPR 2nd Army Corps' brigades was the 10th Separate Artillery Brigade, headquartered in Luhansk. It maintained a much lower signature on open-source media than other LPR brigades, and as such details about it are unclear.

The unit was formed in August 2014, at which time it possessed only eight BM-21 Grad 122mm MLRS and four 2S1 Gvozdika 122mm self-propelled howitzers.[27] Later on in 2014 and into early 2015, the brigade was supplied with more BM-21 Grad MLRS and 2A65 Msta-B towed howitzers.

In addition, it was 'actively supplied' (i.e. by the Russian Federation) with D-30 122mm towed howitzers.[28] The 10th

A poster advertising service in the 6th Separate Motorised Rifle Cossack Regiment. The text reads: 'Serve under contract in the 6th Separate Cossack Motor Rifle Regiment – the cause of true patriots! Have such a profession – Defend the homeland!!!' The picture used for the poster is that of T-72B main battle tanks of the Regiment's tank companies parading in Luhansk on a 9 May parade. (PLPK Stock Photo)

Brigade also received at least one BM-27 Uragan MLRS, captured from Ukrainian forces in 2014, the other captured unit going to the DPR 1st Army Corps Separate Artillery Brigade 'Kalmius.'

By mid-2015 the brigade had been fully equipped, with six BM-27 Uragan MLRS, eighteen BM-21 Grad, eighteen 2S1 Gvozdika and eighteen 2A65 Msta-B systems.[29] Protection for these artillery assets was provided in the form of at least one 9K33 Osa and one 9K35 Strela-10 air defence system.

As the LPR 2nd Army Corps reorganisations got under way, around mid-2015 the brigade received its numbering, becoming the 10th Separate Artillery Brigade. Previously unmarked artillery systems were now painted with a number '10' in a square.

Towards the end of 2015, the brigade was re-equipped with more powerful 2A36 Giatsint-B 152mm towed artillery systems, to counter increasingly powerful artillery being fielded by the Ukrainian Armed Forces. The prime movers for these systems were Ural-632301 8x8 trucks. In 2016, some of these artillery systems were detected by a Ukrainian UAV (unmanned aerial vehicle) in the western part of Luhansk oblast.[30]

6th Separate Motorised Rifle Cossack Regiment named after Matvey Platov (6-й Отдельный Мотострелковый Казачий Полк им. Матвея Платова)

As already discussed above the early Cossack units in the LPR were Kozitsyn's 'Cossack National Guard' which was by far the largest of the Cossack armed formations that sprang up in Ukraine, and the 'First Cossack Regiment' of the Don Cossack Host led by a Pavel Dremov, which splintered off from the Cossack National Guard.

In January 2015, the 'Cossack National Guard' was formally absorbed into the LPR 2nd Army Corps as the 6th Separate Motorised Rifle Cossack Regiment named after Matvey Platov, unit number 69647. The name referred to that of a historical Cossack ataman of the All-Great Don Army, Matvey Platov, who took part in the wars of the Russian Empire during the nineteenth century.

Within the 6th Motorised Rifle Cossack Regiment were at least two tank companies, equipped with T-72B main battle tanks, the 2nd Tank Company paraded in central Luhansk on 9 May 2017.[31]

The 6th Regiment also included an Engineer Sapper Company which was equipped with the UR-77 Meteorit mine-clearing vehicle.[32] The UR-77 Meteorit is mounted on a 2S1 Gvozdika-type chassis (in turn derived from the MT-LB), and clears mines using an explosive line charge thrown up to 90m from the vehicle. The same Engineer Sapper Company within the 6th Regiment also used the smaller UR-83 mine-clearing system.[33]

While otherwise generally equipped in the same fashion as other LPR units, instead of a helmet or beret many Cossack militants in the LPR's Cossack units wore the *papakha*, the wool hat associated with Cossack units of the Russian Empire.

Separate Commandant's Regiment (Отдельный Комендантский Полк)

The LPR's Separate Commandant's Regiment operated under the LPR Ministry of Defence, with unit number 44444. Its logo comprised a large yellow 'K' superimposed on a red shield.

The unit was created in November 2014, and its members took part in a number of battles including the battle for Debaltseve. From April 2014 to March 2015, 46 militants of the regiment were killed and 215 were injured.[34]

Liaising closely with the LPR MGB (State Security Ministry) and Ministry of Internal Affairs, primarily the unit was tasked with protecting important military sites within the LPR, and providing military escort to convoys. Internally it comprised two battalions, a separate guard company, and a mechanised unit.

4th Separate Tank Battalion (4-й Отдельный Танковый Батальон)

Notable among the LPR 2nd Army Corps separate battalions was the 4th Separate Tank Battalion. Formed in late 2014, the unit was initially designated a Separate Mechanised Battalion (OMB) by the name of 'August' (officially the 'Blessed Virgin Mary of August named after Alexander Nevsky'). In early 2015 it was redesignated as the 4th Separate Tank Battalion under the LPR 2nd Army Corps, and lost the 'August' name.[35]

In terms of structure, after it had received its full complement of tanks, there were four tank companies. The 1st company was equipped with T-72B MBTs, and the 2nd, 3rd and 4th companies with T-64.[36] In addition there was a motorised rifle company equipped with BTR-80 APCs, and an artillery *divizion* fielding 2S1 Gvozdika 122mm self-propelled howitzers and BM-21 Grad MLRS.

When it was a Separate Mechanised Battalion, the tactical markings for unit equipment were a hollow white square displaying no number, sometimes with the word 'August' written in close proximity. After being designated the 4th Separate Tank Battalion, the unit marking was a number '8' in a white square. This mismatch between the number of the unit and the marking was presumably to differentiate it from the 4th Separate Motorised Rifle Brigade, as the LPR used squares for all its unit markings irrespective of size.

Territorial defence battalions

In addition to the line brigades and key units listed above, the LPR 2nd Army Corps also incorporated eight territorial defence battalions (батальон территориальной обороны, usually abbreviated in Russian to БТрО or BTrO). Upon the formation of the LPR 2nd Army Corps, some of the early units were split, with one part going into the line brigades and regiments, and another part being placed into a BTrO. The eight BTrOs were as follows:

- 11th territorial defence battalion 'Ataman' (11-й батальон территориальной обороны «Атаман») based in Luhansk.
- 12th territorial defence battalion 'Rome' (12-й батальон территориальной обороны «Рим») unit number 12265 based in Dovzhansk (formerly Sverdlovsk). BTrO 'Rome' was

initially a private militia set up in the city of Dovzhansk, it fought at Debaltseve in 2015 and was later designated as a BTrO. The 12th BTrO suffered heavy casualties during the fighting in February 2022 during the crossing of the Siverskyi Donets River at Trokhizbenka and the subsequent battle for the city of Shchastia, with websites listing numerous members of the battalion who had been killed in action.[37]

- 13th territorial defence battalion 'Kulkin' (13-й Егоровский батальон территориальной обороны «Кулькин») based in Rovenky. The battalion comprised mostly of Cossacks. The battalion commander was killed in an ambush by unknown assailants in October 2016.
- 14th territorial defence battalion 'Prizrak' (14-й батальон территориальной обороны «Призрак») based in Holubivka (formely Kirovsk). The 14th BTrO evidently absorbed some part of the original 'Prizrak' that was not incorporated into the 4th Separate Motorised Rifle Brigade.
- 15th territorial defence battalion 'USSR' (15-й батальон территориальной обороны «СССР») based in Bryanka.
- 16th territorial defence battalion 'Leshy' (16-й батальон территориальной обороны «Леший») based in Antratsyt. As with the 14th BTrO, a result of a splitting of the original 'Leshy' unit, with another part of 'Leshy' ending up in the 4th Separate Motorised Rifle Brigade.
- 17th territorial defence battalion 'Bolshoi' (17-й батальон территориальной обороны «Большой») based in Perevalsk.
- 18th territorial defence battalion 'Pokhodny' (18-й батальон территориальной обороны «Походный») based in Khrustalnyi (formerly Krasni Luch).

LPR armoured fighting vehicles parked outside the city hall in Perevalsk, Luhansk oblast, on 5 November 2014. The T-64BV is marked with the word 'РИМ' ('ROME') associating it with an armed formation set up as a private militia in Dovzhansk and later brought into the LPR 2nd Army Corps as the 12th territorial defence battalion 'Rome' (12-й батальон территориальной обороны «Рим»). To the left of the T-64 are three BMP-2 infantry fighting vehicles, one flying a Russian flag and another the flag of the Don Cossack Host. (Associated Press/Alamy Stock Photo)

Further units of LPR 2nd Army Corps

In addition to the units listed above, the structure of LPR 2nd Army Corps likely comprised the further following units: separate reconnaissance battalion, separate anti-aircraft battalion, separate logistics battalion, separate electronic warfare/SIGINT company, and a separate engineer company.

Additions to LPR 2nd Army Corps units (after Feb 2022)

The DPR and LPR began their mass mobilisation of military personnel in February 2022, a few days before the start of the full-scale Russian invasion of Ukraine. The mobilisation in the LPR was carried out by the Military Commissariat, the organisation in charge of managing mobilisation and conscription. New units were then created from the newly mobilised recruits.

In total, 21 new rifle regiments were formed in the DPR and LPR, with 17 in the DPR 1st Army Corps and four in the LPR 2nd Army Corps. The rifle regiments formed in the LPR were the 202nd, 204th, 206th and 208th.[38] Each of these rifle regiments numbered about 1,500 mobilised individuals, arranged into five battalions per regiment.[39]

These new regiments were then subordinated to the pre-existing line brigades of the LPR 2nd Army Corps. There were widely reported shortages of weapons, body armour and equipment for the newly mobilised members of these units, many of whom were sent to the front with only minimal training. Some were photographed using 7.62mm Mosin–Nagant bolt action rifles, and wearing Second World War-era Soviet helmets.

LPR Military Commissariat subdued patch, c. 2016. (Private collection, used with permission)

There were also complaints of tensions with regular Russian forces: 'In mid-May [2022], a video appeared online of a protest rally held by the wives of combatants from the 206th Regiment of the Luhansk "people's militia." The women, who were demanding a meeting with "LNR" head Leonid Pasechnik, claimed that Russian forces had withdrawn from the Kharkiv region, leaving their husbands in their positions.'[40] Videos on the internet appealed for collections of body armour and other equipment for the LPR 206th rifle regiment in September 2022.[41]

8

ARMED FORMATIONS OF THE LPR NOT FALLING UNDER THE 2ND ARMY CORPS

In addition to the LPR 2nd Army Corps, there were also a number of other armed formations which existed within the territory of the LPR. In particular, these related to two powerful internal ministries within the LPR, namely the Ministry of Internal Affairs and the Ministry of State Security.

The LPR Ministry of State Security saw itself as a descendent of the KGB or NKVD, and deployed MGB units to enforce security within the LPR. This included checking people entering and leaving LPR-controlled territory at the checkpoints. MGB units were usually armed, with personnel carrying light weapons like AK-74s.

The LPR Ministry of Internal Affairs had under its control police units, including the paramilitary OMON units (ОМОН – Отряд Мобильный Особого Назначения, or Special Purpose Mobile Unit). LPR OMON units were called 'Berkut,' after the riot police units that had been disbanded in Ukraine in the aftermath of the Euromaidan protests, and many personnel in them had served in those pre-2014 units. They also recruited from among those who had served in the LPR's armed formations. LPR police units utilised armoured vehicles including armoured Ural 6x6 trucks, and at least one armoured HMMWV most likely captured from Ukrainian forces. Examples of these vehicles were included in the 9 May Victory parade in 2021 which took place in central Luhansk.[1]

LPR MGB subdued patch, c. 2016. The design of the shield and the downward pointing dagger with scrolled handguards, is derived directly from the design of the shield of the KGB/NKVD. (Private collection, used with permission)

9

WEAPONRY AND EQUIPMENT OF THE LPR ARMED FORMATIONS

The weaponry and equipment used by the LPR armed formations evolved over the course of three broad phases. The first phase was that from early to mid-2014, when the nascent armed formations used captured and looted equipment take from Ukrainian government facilities. This included for example small arms stolen from the Ukrainian SBU headquarters in Luhansk, but also included heavier equipment such as several BRDM-2RKh CBRN (Chemical, Biological, Radiological, and Nuclear) reconnaissance vehicles stolen from Ukrainian State Emergency Services compounds in May 2014.[1] In these early days of the conflict in Donbas, the weapons and equipment used by the LPR were very mixed, with small arms including hunting rifles or other privately held weaponry.

The second phase was the long period starting in mid to late 2014, when the supply of military equipment began in earnest from Russia. This supply was informally referred to as 'voentorg,' the Russian word for a military surplus shop, after an infamous comment made by Putin in response to a question as to where the militants in Donbas were getting their equipment from.

Though this is sometimes assumed to have started from the first days of the conflict, in fact it seems that it took the Kremlin some several months to decide to start supplying weaponry – in particular heavy weaponry such as artillery and MBTs – to the LPR in significant quantities, with this supply stream commencing around June 2014. As the various early units such as the 'Army of the South-East' were eventually brought into the LPR 2nd Army Corps, the Kremlin also sought to impose a degree of standardisation in terms of weapon types, vehicles, and uniform.

The types of military equipment supplied to the LPR's armed formations by the Kremlin was designed to maintain the cover of 'plausible deniability' in terms of where the equipment had come from. The Russian government maintained that it provided only humanitarian aid to the LPR, and that the main source of weaponry used by the LPR's armed formations was '…stockpiles inherited by Ukraine in 1991 from the Soviet Army that was formerly tasked to hold off the entire NATO. A lot of these stockpiles were deposited in the old mines of Donbass and later captured by rebels. Another source of weapons was the retreating Ukrainian army itself.'[2]

These claims became increasingly stretched as time went on, as more sophisticated weaponry was seen in the hands of the LPR's armed formations. Investigative journalism websites such as Bellingcat recorded advanced weapons systems in LPR and DPR-controlled areas using open-source research techniques. These claims would then be rebuffed, and the ensuing claim and counter-claim formed part of the intense information warfare that characterised the conflict in Donbas between 2014 and 2022.

In spite of this increasingly flimsy 'deniability,' the supply to the LPR was restricted to certain types corresponding to the late Soviet period of the 1980s and early 1990s. This was particularly true in the areas of main battle tanks, infantry fighting vehicles, armoured personnel carriers and artillery. It is perhaps also worth pointing out that, in parallel to a carefully calibrated pattern of supply designed to create 'deniability,' another factor determining the types of equipment supplied may have been simple cost.

The early-model T-64s and T-72s, and 2S1 Gvozdika howitzers were of types largely retired from service in the regular Russian military. Providing these to the LPR and DPR from deep storage warehouses was undoubtedly cheaper than supplying modern, up-to-date and expensive military equipment. In terms of overall support, including direct financial aid, it was estimated that by 2018 Russia was spending up to $2 billion per year on the LPR and DPR.

The third phase corresponded with the start of the full-scale Russian invasion of Ukraine commencing in February 2022. In the first days after 24 February, Russian military commentators noted that the 'irregular' LPR and DPR forces would have to be re-equipped with modern military equipment when fully integrated into Russian conventional forces. However, as the full-scale invasion got under way and Russian losses mounted, the capacity for the Russian military to equip the LPR or DPR with modern equipment diminished, as it diverted such supplies to replace losses among its own units.

This section will examine the weaponry and equipment that was used by the LPR's armed formations, based on open-source research. An area of difficulty, in particular during the second phase from late 2014 to early 2022, is clearly differentiating between the LPR's armed formations and those regular Russian units deployed to Donbas.

In late 2014 and early 2015, as has been discussed above, such regular Russian units were deployed in force as part of the 'Northern Wind' to prevent the LPR from total military defeat. Later on, it was usually as smaller units of particular technical function, such as electronic warfare. This careful blending of 'irregular' LPR and regular Russian forces was part of a careful strategy. As this book's primary focus is on the LPR's armed formations, it will discuss those equipment types reliably documented in use by the LPR.

Small arms

In the first days of the conflict, the LPR's early armed formations used a wide variety of small arms. Some were drawn from civilian hunting and shooting groups, military re-enactment groups, and even museums. The LPR's early armed formations, in particular the 'Army of the South-East,' also secured a significant supply of small arms when they stormed the SBU headquarters in Luhansk.

Over time, as the Kremlin began to reorganise the early units into the LPR 2nd Army Corps, these small arms were replaced by the 5.45mm AK-74 assault rifle and variants, in particular the modernised AK-74M. This became the standard infantry weapon for units of the LPR 2nd Army Corps. Older versions of the AK, such as the 7.62mm AKM, remained in service with the LPR police.

The LPR's armed formations also made use of support weapons such as the 5.54x39mm RPK-74 light machine gun and the 7.62x54mmR PK and PKM general purpose machine gun.

Heavy machine guns included the 12.7×108mm DShK and 12.7x108mm NSV.

7.62×54mmR SVDM and SVDS sniper rifles and 9mm VSS Vintorez were used by LPR armed formations. The 9mm silenced Vintorez rifle was pictured in use by the LPR's 'Vityaz' battalion.[3]

A T-72B main battle tank driving through Sorokyne (formerly Krasnodon) in Luhansk oblast on 17 August 2014. This vehicle was part of a column of several dozen heavy vehicles, including tanks and at least one rocket launcher, observed by Associated Press reporters in Sorokyne on that date. Close to the Russian border, Sorokyne was a likely transit hub for military equipment moving across the border into the LPR, the so-called 'voentorg.' (Associated Press/Alamy Stock Photo)

The Vintorez was about 10 times more expensive than a normal SVD-type sniper rifle. Over the static contact line between 2015 and 2022, sniping was one of the main forms of warfare, and by 2020 it was estimated that approximately a third of all Ukrainian military casualties were being caused by sniper fire.[4]

Anti-tank and light support weapons

Light anti-tank weapons were of particular importance to the LPR's armed formations in 2014, as a means of countering the mechanised units of the Ukrainian military. As the LPR armed formations grew in size in early 2014, there was at first an acute shortage of weaponry. Various examples of the PTRS-41 and PTRD-41 anti-tank rifles, firing the 14.5×114mm armour-piercing round were removed from local museums, or otherwise entered into service with the LPR. Despite their Second World War heritage, these weapons remained useful as anti-materiel weapons, and were used against vehicles and light armour. The ammunition for the weapons was the same as that used in the KPVT machine gun mounted in the turret of the BTR-60/70/80 armoured personnel carriers, or the BRDM-2 reconnaissance vehicle.

Igor 'Strelkov' Girkin apparently expressed an opinion that the PTRD-41 was the more reliable of the two weapons, and wished there had been more of them.[5] Even as more modern anti-tank weapons began to arrive in greater quantities, the PTRD and PTRS-41 remained in service with the LPR as the conflict in Donbas went on.

In terms of more modern anti-tank weaponry, single-shot RPG types like the RPG-22 and RPG-26 were soon in common use. In addition the RPG-7 rocket-propelled grenade launcher was also distributed, despite its age. Further anti-armour capability was provided by weapons systems such as the Soviet-era 9K113 Konkurs SACLOS wire-guided anti-tank missile. It was well suited to the static warfare across the contact line, being less portable and more suited to defensive operations. Another Soviet-era weapons system, the tripod-mounted SPG-9 Kopye 73mm recoilless gun was also a common weapon across LPR units.

Using trucks or MT-LB armoured personnel carriers as prime movers, the MT-12 Rapira 100m Soviet-era towed anti-tank gun was present among LPR units, nominally as an anti-tank weapon. Given its questionable utility against modern Ukrainian main battle tanks, it saw more service as a light artillery piece. The even older BS-3 100mm towed anti-tank gun was also used by the LPR in limited numbers, with one example exhibited in 'Patriot Park.'

Other infantry support weapons included the AGS-17 Plamya and AGS-30 30mm automatic grenade launchers, as well as 82mm and 120mm mortars. The 2B9 Vasilek 82mm automatic gun-mortar was also in service.

Another weapon used by LPR armed formations was the RPO-A Shmel single-shot rocket launched thermobaric weapon. Such a weapon, for example, was reportedly found by Ukrainian security forces in 2018 in the home of a wanted LPR militant living in (Ukrainian controlled) Lysychansk.[6]

Landmines

The LPR made extensive use of anti-tank landmines, especially during the static period of the conflict from 2015 to early 2022. Metal body TM-62M and plastic body TM-62P3 anti-tank mines were commonly used, usually in defensive belts laid on the surface. Research done by OSINT websites demonstrated that at least some of the mines in use by the armed formations of the DPR and LPR were made after 1991 in factories in Russia.[7]

Both sides in the conflict in Donbas made extensive use of anti-tank landmines, for the purposes of obstructing or channelling enemy movement. This became especially prevalent as the contact line solidified and both sides dug-in to static positions with little movement.

Further landmine types emplaced by the LPR included OZM-72 bounding fragmentation mines, which were common in the area around the Stanytsia Luhanska bridges, as well as on the banks of the Siverskyi Donets River. MON-50, MON-90 and MON-100 directional fragmentation mines were also used.

Main battle tanks

Initially, the early armed formations of the LPR were badly overmatched by the mechanised units of the Ukrainian armed forces. Despite the capture of a few armoured vehicles, such as BRDM-RKh CBRN reconnaissance vehicles, the armed formations of the LPR had no answer to the mechanised forces deployed by Ukraine which began recapturing territory in the north of Luhansk oblast. It was not until June 2014 that the first T-64s and T-72s began appearing in the hands of the LPR and DPR.

The appearance of these main battle tanks in the LPR's armed formations signified a major escalation of the conflict. From June 2014 onwards, the LPR was soon fielding significant numbers of T-64 main battle tanks, far more than could have been captured from Ukrainian forces. Equally important was the evident presence of a covert yet extensive supply and logistics chain helping to keep these fuel and maintenance hungry vehicles functional.

The LPR mostly fielded the T-64BV, an upgraded version of the T-64B featuring Kontakt-1 explosive reactive armour on the glacis plate, side skirts and turret. Earlier T-64B variants were also present. The T-64 had been inherited by the armed forces of both Ukraine and the Russian Federation after the dissolution of the Soviet Union.

However, it retained more significance in Ukraine, as the Kharkiv Morozov Machine-building Design Bureau was located in newly-independent Ukraine, where the T-64 had been designed and built. This had allowed Ukraine to continue maintaining and developing the T-64. It was for this reason that T-64s were supplied to the LPR armed formations, in keeping with the desire to maintain a pretence of 'plausible deniability.'

Nevertheless, the LPR did capture at least a few T-64s from the Ukrainian armed forces. Most notably, these included at least a couple of examples of the T-64 Bulat variant, a deep modernisation of the T-64 developed by Ukraine in 2004. A couple of examples of these tanks were captured by the LPR and used by one of their early units, 'Odessa.'[8]

The LPR also received a supply of T-72s from Russia. These were an even clearer indicator of Russian military supply, as Ukraine had standardised its tank forces around the T-64 owing to the previously mentioned presence of the main production and repair facility in Kharkiv. At the time the conflict started in Donbas, there were only 200–300 older model T-72s remaining in Ukraine, most of these in deep storage in central or western Ukraine. None of these were combat-ready when the fighting erupted in the east of Ukraine.

The models supplied to the LPR were primarily the T-72B and T-72B1, but there were also limited numbers of the more advanced T-72B Model 1989, identified in service with the 'Cossack National Guard.'[9] The T-72B Model 1989 was visually very different to the T-72B and T-72B1, having triangular Kontakt-5 explosive reactive armour blocks around the turret, and modular Kontakt-5 on the glacis plate.

In addition, some open-source research suggested that the LPR had received some examples of the T-72S1, an export version of the T-72B1 supplied by Russia to Iran and Venezuela.[10] These T-72S1s were recorded in service with the LPR's 4th Separate Motorised Rifle Brigade. The visual differences with the T-72B1 were small, with a different night sight and a wind sensor mount. Though Russian supply of tanks and infantry fighting vehicles was designed to mimic types that might conceivably had been captured from Ukraine, this usually applied only to the base model.

Following the start of the full-scale Russian invasion of Ukraine in February 2022, the LPR's expanded armed formations began to receive T-62M main battle tanks. Footage on social media showed LPR T-62M tanks moving towards Lysychansk in June 2022, with improvised cages built above the turrets.[11]

Infantry fighting vehicles and armoured personnel carriers

The mainstay tracked infantry fighting vehicles used by the LPR 2nd Army Corps motorised rifle brigades were the BMP-1 and BMP-2 infantry fighting vehicles.

A T-72B main battle tank parked in Teatralnaya Ploshchad (Theatre Square) on the day before parliamentary elections for the Luhansk People's Republic, November 2014. This detailed study of the front of the T-72B shows Kontakt-1 explosive reactive armour (ERA) blocks on the turret roof, turret front and glacis plate. The TPD-K1 gunner's sight is above the driver, and also visible is the circular L-2AG Luna-2 infrared spotlight, mounted to the right of the 125 mm main gun. (Iva Zimova/Panos Pictures)

LPR armoured vehicles form a convoy as they roll along the streets of Kadiivka (formerly Stakhanov) in Luhansk oblast on 24 April 2015. The MT-LB was the standard tracked armoured personnel carrier across the LPR 2nd Army Corps. This example, and the three BMP-1 infantry fighting vehicles behind it, are marked with a '4' in a white square, denoting them as belonging to the LPR 4th Separate Motorised Rifle Brigade. (Associated Press/Alamy Stock Photo)

These were used in standard configuration, with some being equipped with rubber side skirts or similar improvised armour. The more modern BMP-3 infantry fighting vehicles were not supplied by the Kremlin's 'voentorg', in keeping with the restricted supply of late Soviet equipment.

The tracked MT-LB and wheeled BTR-60, BTR-70 and BTR-80 APCs saw common use in the LPR 2nd Army Corps. The versatile MT-LB was also used as a prime mover for towed artillery, such as the MT-12 Rapira, as well as a carrier platform for ZU-23-2 anti-aircraft cannon. Many modifications of the MT-LB were observed, including the addition of cage armour, or additional armour plates to provide extra protection to the crew compartment.

The LPR also conducted some improvised modifications of MT-LBs, using them as a platform for BMP-1 turrets. Social media posts which depicted these vehicles showed non-standard and clearly very improvised designs, with the turret placed in one instance close to the centre of the MT-LB, and in another instance closer to the rear.[12] Additional protection was provided by lattice or cage armour. Markings on the vehicles depicted a number '6' in a white square, associating them with the 6th Separate Motorised Rifle Cossack Regiment.

One wheeled armoured vehicle used by the LPR was the UAZ-23632-148 Esaul vehicle, the presence of which was first reliably confirmed in the neighbouring DPR in April 2021.[13] The vehicle was then seen on parade during the 2021 Victory Day parade in Luhansk on 9 May, armed with AGS-17 automatic grenade launchers and 12.7mm DShK machineguns, and described as belonging to an 'anti-sniper' unit.[14] Built by the Russian company UAZ to include such features as armoured fuel tanks and a dedicated weapons ring

mount in the cargo bed, the vehicle was a formalised incarnation of the 'technicals' seen in many contemporary conflicts. At least 15 of these modern vehicles were thought to have been supplied to the LPR by Russia.

Artillery

After the conflict line solidified between 2015 and 2022, artillery became one of the most important weapons systems possessed by the LPR. Artillery duelling was a common type of fighting that flared up around the contact line 'hotspots' in Luhansk oblast. During that period, it was estimated that approximately 80 percent of all the casualties (military and civilian) on both sides of the conflict were caused by artillery fire.[15]

The LPR was well-equipped with the 2S1 Gvozdika 122mm self-propelled howitzers, most held within the 10th Separate Artillery Brigade. This versatile self-propelled artillery piece proved eminently suitable to the conflict in Donbas, having the benefit of being relatively low maintenance.

In early September 2014, two 2S3 Akatsia 152mm self-propelled howitzers were captured by the LPR at Perevalsk from the Ukrainian 1st Separate Guards Tank Brigade.[16] There was little evidence though that the LPR actually used these vehicles later. It is possible one of the captured 2S3s was the vehicle later displayed at the LPR's 'Patriot Park' on the runway of the former Luhansk International Airport.

One unusual self-propelled artillery piece developed by the LPR was a 2S9 Nona 120mm mortar system mounted on an MT-LB chassis.[17] This was apparently built using a captured 2S9 Nona whose chassis had either been damaged or otherwise rendered nonfunctional.

Towed artillery included D-30 122mm towed howitzers, 2A65 Msta-B systems and later the more powerful 2A36 Giatsint-B 152mm towed artillery systems. The 2S19 Msta-S was never identified in LPR service, meaning that the LPR's 152mm artillery capability was in the form of towed systems only.

The mainstay multiple launch rocket system was the BM-21 Grad 122mm MLRS, with the longer range BM-27 Uragan 220mm MLRS also present in smaller numbers.

Air defence systems

Initially, as the Ukrainian ATO started to roll back territorial gains made by the nascent LPR, the Ukrainian military was able to utilise airpower to great effect. The early LPR armed formations had no answer to this, possessing no airpower of their own, and no real anti-aircraft systems except small arms and heavy machineguns.

Despite providing massive military support in other areas, in 2014 and 2015 Russia remained unwilling to provide support in the form of using its own air force over eastern Ukraine. This was probably because it deemed doing so would stretch its 'plausible deniability' in the eyes of the international community too far.

Instead, the LPR began to receive a number of anti-aircraft systems, which quickly began to have an effect on the battlefield. At first, starting around May or June 2014, supply was of MANPADS in the form of the 9K38 Igla and 9K32 Strela-2. An Igla system was most likely used by LPR militants to shoot down the Ukrainian Il-76 near Luhansk Airport on 14 June 2014.[18]

This singular loss, plus mounting losses of other aircraft to MANPADS wielded by the LPR and DPR, effectively caused the Ukrainian armed forces to cease using crewed military aircraft for combat operations in Donbas by around August 2014. MANPADS these had the effect of negating the Ukrainian advantage in combat airpower, which the LPR and DPR could not directly match.

The twin-barrelled ZU-23-2 23mm towed anti-aircraft cannon was also widely used by the LPR, either mounted in fortifications or placed on the back of trucks and MT-LBs. They were however generally utilised in a ground-to-ground role.

Later in 2014, more advanced air defence systems started to arrive within LPR armed formations. These included primarily the 9K35 Strela-10, comprising a highly mobile system on an MT-LB chassis, and numerous examples of the wheeled 9K33 Osa air defence system. The presence of the 9K33 Osa was one area where the LPR seemed in contrast to the DPR, with whom 9K33 Osa systems were rarely documented, and never openly paraded.

Supporting these air defence systems was the use of a chain of air defence radars across DPR and LPR territory, with each radar set back around 20 or 30km from the contact line. These evidently formed some kind of integrated air defence system covering the entire length of the LPR and DPR front line, and the radars were in place for many years, such that they were actually easily visible on commercial satellite imagery.[19]

In early 2021, an advanced Russian-made 51U6 Kasta-2E1 target and acquisition radar was identified in Luhansk, close to the city of Alchevsk. This was a more advanced system than the Soviet-era P-15 or P-19 surveillance and target acquisition radars hitherto identified in DPR-controlled territory. However, the extent to which the air defence radar system was actually operated by the LPR is a matter of debate, more likely it was part of direct military support from Russia.

In addition to these ground-based radars, the Russian air force would sometimes fly a Beriev A-50 early warning and control aircraft up and down the Russian side of the border over Rostov oblast. Such an aircraft would have been able to cover eastern Ukraine including the DPR and LPR without leaving Russian airspace.

A month after the downing of the Ukrainian armed forces Il-76 near Luhansk Airport, Malaysian Airlines MH17 was shot down over Donbas on 17 July 2014, most probably by a 9K37 Buk system which fired at the airliner from DPR-controlled territory near the town of Snizhne in Donetsk oblast.[20]

Amid the international outrage at the downing of MH-17, the then-commander of the Cossack National Guard, Kozitsyn, was heard in a leaked telephone conversation discussing the crash site.[21] In a follow-up interview he did not deny he had been discussing the shooting down of the airliner, but declined to comment on who had done it.[22]

The 9K37 Buk system allegedly involved in the downing of MH-17 was rapidly withdrawn into Russia and disappeared, and an aggressive information warfare campaign promoted various 'competing theories' about what had happened to the airliner in order to shift blame. Perhaps in this attempt to limit reputational damage, no 9K37 Buk system was ever paraded by the LPR or DPR, or reliably documented in their possession.

A Cossack stands guard at an LPR base in Perevalsk, 5 November 2014. He wears a *berezhka* (birch tree) camouflage pattern combat uniform and *papakha* hat, and carries an AKM 7.62mm assault rifle. The cockade on the hat is in the Russian Imperial pattern. In the background is a 2S3 Akatsia 152mm self-propelled howitzer, likely one of two captured by the LPR in September 2014 from the Ukrainian 1st Separate Guards Tank Brigade. (Associated Press/Alamy Stock Photo)

An LPR militant poses for a colleague while standing on the running board of a BM-21 Grad 122mm MLRS parked in Teatralnaya Ploshchad (Theatre Square) on the day before parliamentary elections for the Luhansk People's Republic in November 2014. The pair wear VSR-98 'Flora' camouflage combat uniforms and carry AK-74M 5.45mm assault rifles. (Iva Zimova/Panos Pictures)

An LPR militant takes part in a training exercise in a field 30km from Luhansk city, 14 April 2016. The weapon is a 9K38 Igla MANPADS. (Xinhua/Alamy Stock Photo)

Aircraft

Fixed wing and rotary crewed-aircraft were notably absent from the capabilities of both the LPR and DPR. Factors which probably influenced this decision may have included the lack of personnel skilled enough to fly and maintain such craft, plus their likely limited military effectiveness when deployed in small numbers, and faced with the numerous Ukrainian air defence systems across Donbas.

A video posted by the LPR 'Leshy' battalion depicted a number of aircraft at a small airfield in 2014.[23] In the video, LPR militants from 'Leshy' start a Yak-52 aerobatic trainer aircraft and fly around in it, but the other aircraft at the airfield (including an Aero L-29 Delfin jet trainer) were clearly not flightworthy.

The LPR did parade an Su-25 attack aircraft on its 9 May Victory Day parades in central Luhansk,[24] but this was purely for propaganda purposes as the aircraft depicted in a number of online videos was never used in any combat operation and most likely not flightworthy.[25]

After 2014, which saw the loss of a number of Ukrainian military aircraft to MANPADs and other air defence systems (discussed above), neither side used any crewed aircraft in the skies directly above the contact line, for either reconnaissance or offensive operations. The use of combat airpower over Donbas, mostly for close air support, only commenced again upon the full-scale invasion of February 2022.

UAVs

After the battle for Debaltseve and the signing of Minsk II, the contact line stabilised in Luhansk oblast and barely changed over the next seven years. During this time, the use of UAVs rapidly expanded, as tools for reconnaissance, artillery fire correction, and also as a means of delivering ordnance onto targets.

The LPR had access to two types of UAVs: commercial off-the-shelf models, and Russian-made military UAVs. Relatively cheap and available commercial off-the-shelf quadcopter drones were probably the most widely used. These performed reconnaissance and target correction roles, and as the conflict went on, some were modified to drop small munitions onto targets.

Various Russian-made military UAVs were also identified in Donbas from 2014 to 2022, including the Granat-1, Granat-2, Granat-4, Forpost, Orlan-10, Eleron-3SV, Zastava, and Tachyon systems.[26] As an example, a Navodchik-2 artillery reconnaissance system was identified in LPR-controlled territory in November 2020, comprising a control centre mounted on a KamAZ-4350 chassis capable of launching several Granat-family UAVs.[27]

The extent to which more advanced Russian-made UAV systems were actually operated by the LPR is unclear. Some Ukrainian sources suggest that the LPR 2nd Army Corps directly operated Orlan-10, Eleron-3, and Tachyon systems, with the Separate Reconnaissance Battalion utilising these types, as well as the 2nd and 4th Motorised Rifle Brigades.[28] Other systems were more likely operate by specialised Russian units operating in Luhansk oblast.

LPR militants ride on a truck being driven on a parade in Luhansk city, 14 September 2014. The weapon mounted on the back of the truck is a ZU-23-2 23mm anti-aircraft cannon, and the crew member sitting closest to the camera appears to be holding an RPK light machinegun. Spraypainted on the bullet-damaged side of truck is the Russian word for 'Trophy' suggesting it had been captured from Ukrainian forces. On the far left of the picture is a religious themed flag, with a depiction of Christ against a red background. (Associated Press/Alamy Stock Photo)

Forms of communications jamming, as well as GPS jamming or spoofing, slowly became prevalent across the contact line area, in particular around the known 'flashpoints.' Despite a few references to an LPR 2nd Army Corps Electronic Warfare Company, it is most likely that Russian regular military personnel operated such advanced electronic warfare systems directly, liaising with the LPR armed formations.

Tracked transporters, trucks and light vehicles

One area where Russia supplied military equipment to the LPR with little consideration to 'deniability' was in the form of military trucks. Newer version of the Ural-4320 6x6 truck rapidly became common across the LPR's armed formations,

Electronic warfare

The development of a layered air defence system by the LPR has already been discussed, which had the effect of preventing the use of crewed aircraft over the contact line by the Ukrainian armed forces. However, these Soviet-style air defence systems were of limited use against the growing Ukrainian use of cheap and small UAVs.

In order to counter the use of UAVs, electronic warfare systems were deployed by the LPR, DPR and Russia in Donbas in increasing numbers. Donbas was also used as a testing ground for new Russian electronic warfare systems, with systems including the RB-341V Leer-3 and RB-636 Svet-KU identified across the region over the years between 2015 and 2022.[29]

and were distinguished from older versions by an enlarged engine compartment and large black cylindrical air-filter on the passenger side of the bonnet. The LPR modified some of these using improvised armour to create armoured personnel carriers. The Ural-43206 was an even newer military variant in 4x4 configuration, and thus was even easier to distinguish having one fewer axle.

These new military trucks complemented a wide variety of older model Ural and KamAZ trucks which the LPR utilised for day-to-day logistics duties. The smaller GAZ-66 was also present in large numbers, including as a prime mover for towed mortars.

In terms of lighter vehicles, Soviet-era vehicle types like the UAZ-469 jeep and UAZ-452 minivan were in common use. For

Newer-model Ural-4320 and KamAZ trucks in service with the 4th Separate Motorised Rifle Brigade. (PLPK Stock Photo)

some reason, the GAZ-2330 Tigr, in wide service with the Russian military, was not supplied to the LPR or DPR.

A more unusual vehicle that featured in the arsenal of the LPR 2nd Army Corps was the PTS-2 amphibious tracked transporter. A development of the PTS amphibious transporter, the PTS-2 was developed and built in the early 1970s at the Luhansk Diesel Locomotive Factory, based on components from the T-64 main battle tank. Six of these machines remained in the factory in the summer of 2014, when they were seized by militants from the LPR's 'Batman' battalion.[30] Further PTS-2 vehicles were then supplied to the LPR by Russia, and they were used by the LPR 4th Separate Motorised Rifle Brigade.[31]

One absolutely unique vehicle utilised by the LPR 2nd Army Corps was a single example of an amphibious vehicle called the MOP (Машина обеспечения переправ, crossing support vehicle). Developed in the 1980s in Luhansk on the chassis of a PTS-3 amphibious tracked carrier, the vehicle included an MT-LB style turret with 7.62mm PKT machinegun, excavator arm, bulldozer blade, winch, and other equipment to support amphibious crossing.[32]

The purpose of the MOP was to cross to the opposite side of a river and excavate the banks to allow pontoon bridges to be laid. Designed during Soviet times as an experimental model, it never went into serial production. Seized by the LPR in 2014 and returned to working condition, it was regularly paraded on the 9 May Victory Day parades.

Uniforms

In the first year of the conflict, a wide variety of uniforms were observed among LPR armed formation units. During the first months, many militants who occupied Ukrainian government buildings were wearing civilian clothes, with perhaps only St George's ribbons to denote them as a member of an armed group. Soviet-era camouflage uniform was common in early armed formation units, with variants of the 1970s-era 'berezhka' (birch

tree) camouflage uniform and the 1990s VSR-98 'Flora' also known as 'Arbuz' (meaning watermelon) patterns also being widespread.

When these units began to be organised into the LPR 2nd Army Corps, uniforms based on the 2008 Russian EMR 'digital flora' pattern became standard. During winter months, the black and brown Gorka suit was widely used, as well as snow camouflage patterns based on the klyaksa (ink blot) pattern.

Unit patches however seemed rare among LPR units, especially when deployed in the field where only an LPR shield and perhaps a Novorossiya flag might be displayed, if anything. The DPR brigades each had detailed associated symbology in the form of unit patches, in both full colour and subdued variants. This did not seem to be prevalent in the LPR 2nd Army Corps, and as noted above, what unit symbology there was in the LPR was generally at the battalion level.

Medals

The LPR issued a number of medals and awards. The top medal in the LPR was the Hero of the Lugansk People's Republic. This medal mirrored the Hero of the Donetsk People's Republic, and both were directly copied from the Hero of the Soviet Union award. The medal itself comprised a five-pointed gold star, below a ribbon depicting the LPR flag colours of pale blue, dark blue and red. The first recipient of the award was the commander of the 6th Separate Guards Cossack Motorised Rifle Regiment.

There were a number of other LPR medals including those 'For Merit' and 'For Courage.' Unlike the DPR, the LPR did not issue a series of metals for participation in specific battles, with the exception of the 'Battle for Lugansk 2014' medal, which counted Igor Plotnitsky among its recipients.

LPR flag subdued patch, c. 2018. This tactical version of the flag reduced the three bands of colour on the LPR flag to thin lines. (Private collection, used with permission)

An LPR infantryman patrolling in a ruined village somewhere in the LPR, 3 February 2022. After 2016, most LPR uniforms were standardised around the 2008 Russian EMR 'digital flora' pattern. He carries an AK-74M 5.45mm assault rifle, also standard LPR issue. (Abaca Press/Alamy Stock Photo)

10
CONCLUSION

From chaotic beginnings, the groups of violent protestors who stormed Ukrainian government buildings in 2014 were eventually formed by the Kremlin into the LPR 2nd Army Corps, one of its two proxy forces in eastern Ukraine.

Russia's seizure of the Crimean peninsula sparked off the conflict in Donbas, encouraging many pro-Russian Ukrainians to rise up against the state. Their numbers were soon bolstered by Russian volunteers, as well as others from further afield. The ideological motivators for LPR militants were incredibly diverse, and often contradictory. Cossack groups in the territory nominally controlled by the LPR added an additional dimension of complexity, with many such groups not even recognising the authority of the LPR authorities in Luhansk.

For its part, as the violent uprisings in Donbas started in 2014, the Kremlin seemed to vacillate between differing levels of political and military support to the LPR, unwilling to fully support annexation into Russia, but equally unwilling to allow the LPR to be defeated militarily. This came as a disappointment to many initial LPR supporters, who had fully expected a rapid and confident Crimean-style annexation.

Out of this uncertainty came the factional infighting, often violent, which dogged both the People's Republics in eastern Ukraine. This was particularly true of the LPR, where numerous military commanders and politicians were killed in assassinations or removed to Russia over the course of the years from 2014 to 2022.

Supporting the two People's Republics was not without cost to Russia. The LPR's economy was further damaged by asset stripping, as whole factories were quietly shipped away or sold off for scrap. With economies that had been damaged by the conflict, and unable to attract any meaningful external investment, both the LPR and DPR required massive yearly injections of cash to keep them afloat. The cost was estimated in 2018 to be around $2 billion per year, of 0.25 percent of Russian GDP.[1] These costs were in addition to the significant resources Russia had to expend to equip and train the 1st and 2nd Army Corps.

On 24 February 2022, Putin's massive 'special military operation' began. One of its stated goals was to force Ukraine to recognise the independence of the DPR and LPR within the pre-2014 Donetsk and Luhansk oblast boundaries to which each People's Republic had respectively laid claim, and to 'protect the people of Donbas.'

Backed by this Russian military support, for a brief period from July to September 2022 the LPR appeared to have achieved one of the only goals that most of its disparate groups and military leaders could agree on, exercising administrative control over all of Luhansk oblast.

The LPR had however paid a heavy price for this achievement. Frontal assaults on heavily fortified Ukrainian positions, and urban fighting in the dense conurbations of Popasna, Sievierodonetsk and Lysychansk, coupled to the inexperience of many of the fresh conscripts mobilised only in February 2022 had caused high attrition rates among the LPR 2nd Army Corps. Many of the cities captured during the fighting, such as Shchastia and Sievierodonetsk, had been massively damaged by shelling and urban warfare, accompanied by a horrific toll of civilian casualties.

On 30 September 2022, after a carefully choreographed Kremlin-orchestrated referendum, the DPR and LPR were both formally annexed by Russia and vanished as nominally independent political and military entities. Russia's troubled eight-year experiment using proxy forces in eastern Ukraine had come to an abrupt end. Shortly afterwards, on 31 December 2022, the 1st and 2nd Army Corps were formally brought into the Russian military, with Putin presiding over an official ceremony at Rostov-on-Don.

At the time of writing, the future of Donbas is still very much in question, with a Ukrainian counter-offensive underway in the east of the country. In what has widened into a much broader and far more violent conflict between Ukraine and Russia, the troubled origins of what are usually dismissed as 'Russia's proxies' in eastern Ukraine can be easily overlooked. Protection of these proxies formed a large part of Putin's justification for the Kremlin's full-scale invasion of February 2022, resulting in massive loss of life and widespread destruction across Ukraine.

BIBLIOGRAPHY

Books

Arutunyan, Anna, *Hybrid Warriors: Proxies, Freelancers and Moscow's Struggle for Ukraine* (London: Hurst, 2022)

Caspersen, Nina, *Unrecognized States* (Cambridge: Polity, 2012)

Clover, Charles, *Black Wind, White Snow – The rise of Russia's new nationalism* (New Haven: Yale University Press, 2016)

Freedman, Lawrence, *Ukraine and the Art of Strategy* (Oxford: Oxford University Press, 2019)

Kofman, Michael, Migacheva, Katya, Nichiporuk, Brian, Radin, Andrew, Tkacheva, Olesya and Oberholtzer, Jenny, *Lessons from Russia's Operations in Crimea and Eastern Ukraine* (RAND Corporation, 2017)

Overy, Richard, *Russia's War* (1999 e-book edition)

Matveeva, Anna, *Through Times of Trouble – Conflict in Southeastern Ukraine Explained from Within* (Lexington Books, 2018)

Medvedev, Sergei, *The Return of the Russian Leviathan* (Cambridge: Polity, 2020)

Menon, Rajan and Rumer, Eugene, *Conflict in Ukraine – The unwinding of the post-Cold War order* (MIT, 2015)

Monaghan, Andrew, *Russian Grand Strategy in the era of global power competition* (Manchester: Manchester University Press 2022)

Mumford, Andrew, *Proxy Warfare* (Cambridge: Polity Press, 2013)

Puri, Samir, *Russia's Road to War with Ukraine* (London: Biteback Publishing, 2022)

Shevchenko, Artem, *Slovyansk: The Beginning of the War* (Kharkiv: Folio 2020)

Sutyagin, Igor and Bronk, Justin, *Russia's New Ground Forces: Capabilities, Limitations and Implications for International Security* (Abingdon: Routledge 2017)

Swain, Adam (ed.), *Re-constructing the Post-Soviet Industrial Region: The Donbas in transition* (Cambridge: Cambridge University Press 2007)

Wood, Tony, *Russia Without Putin: Money, Power and the Myths of the New Cold War* (London: Verso, 2020)

Yaffa, Joshua, *Between Two Fires – Truth, ambition and compromise in Putin's Russia* (Granta uncorrected bound proof 2020)

Yekelchyk, Serhy, *The Conflict in Ukraine* (Oxford: Oxford University Press, 2015)

Journal articles

Abibok, Yulia, 'On the way to creating the 'Donbas people' – Identity policy in the self-proclaimed republics in east Ukraine', *OSW Commentary*, number 270 (June 2018)

Anon, 'Peace in Ukraine (III): The Costs of War in Donbas', *International Crisis Group*, Report No. 261 (3 Sept 2020), https://www.crisisgroup.org/europe-central-asia/eastern-europe/ukraine/261-peace-ukraine-iii-costs-war-donbas

Kolstø, Pål, 'Symbol of the War — But Which One? The St George Ribbon in Russian Nation-Building', *The Slavonic and East European Review*, Vol. 94, No. 4 (October 2016), pp. 665-666, https://doi.org/10.5699/slaveasteurorev2.94.4.0660

Laruelle, Marlene, 'The three colors of Novorossiya, or the Russian nationalist mythmaking of the Ukrainian crisis', *Post-Soviet Affairs* (2016), 32:1, DOI: 10.1080/1060586X.2015.1023004

Loshkariov, Ivan D., and Sushentsov, Andrey A., 'Radicalization of Russians in Ukraine: from 'accidental' diaspora to rebel movement', *Southeast European and Black Sea Studies*, 16:1 (2016), pp. 71-90, DOI: 10.1080/14683857.2016.1149349

Malyarenko, Tetyana and Galbreath, David J., Paramilitary motivation in Ukraine: beyond integration and abolition, *Southeast European and Black Sea Studies*, 16:1 (2016), pp. 113-138, DOI: 10.1080/14683857.2016.1148414

NOTES

Introduction

1 Oblast – the first unit of territorial sub-division in Ukraine, roughly equivalent to a UK county or US state.

2 Andrew Mumford, *Proxy Warfare* (Cambridge: Polity Press, 2013), chapter 1.

3 Tetyana Malyarenko and David J. Galbreath, 'Paramilitary motivation in Ukraine: beyond integration and abolition', *Southeast European and Black Sea Studies*, 16:1 (2016), pp. 113–138, DOI: 10.1080/14683857.2016.1148414; p. 115

4 Address by the President of the Russian Federation, 24 February 2022

5 As an example: 'Rhetoric is changed in ORDiLO', *Ukrainian Week* website, 2019, https://ukrainianweek.com/Society/232471.

6 Luhansk oblast, Internet Encyclopedia of Ukraine, https://www.encyclopediaofukraine.com/default.asp, accessed 1 June 2023.

7 Nina Caspersen, *Unrecognized States* (Cambridge: Polity, 2012), p. 6

8 Yulia Abibok, 'On the way to creating the 'Donbas people' – Identity policy in the self-proclaimed republics in east Ukraine', *OSW Commentary*, number 270 (June 2018), p. 6

9 This difference in spelling originates in the differing transliterations from Ukrainian and Russian. Similar differences are observed in the spelling of the Ukrainian capital Kyiv (Ukrainian language) vs Kiev (Russian language); and Odesa (Ukrainian language) vs Odessa (Russian language).

Chapter 1

1 Serhy Yekelchyk, *The Conflict in Ukraine* (oxford: Oxford University Press, 2015), p. 5

2 Tony Wood, *Russia Without Putin: Money, Power and the Myths of the New Cold War* (London: Verso, 2020), p. 117

3 Wood, *Russia Without Putin: Money, Power and the Myths of the New Cold War*, p. 7

4 'Bucharest Summit Declaration – Issued by the Heads of State and Government participating in the meeting of the North Atlantic Council in Bucharest on 3 April 2008', NATO website, https://www.nato.int/cps/en/natolive/official_texts_8443.htm

5 Samir Puri, *Russia's Road to War with Ukraine* (London: Biteback Publishing, 2022), p.xv

6 Wood, *Russia Without Putin: Money, Power and the Myths of the New Cold War*, p. 131

7 Anna Arutunyan, *Hybrid Warriors: Proxies, Freelancers and Moscow's Struggle for Ukraine* (London: Hurst, 2022), p. 20

8 Puri, *Russia's Road to War with Ukraine*, p. 6

9 Rajan Menon and Eugene Rumer, *Conflict in Ukraine – The unwinding of the post-Cold War order* (MIT 2015), p. 11

10 Arutunyan, *Hybrid Warriors: Proxies, Freelancers and Moscow's Struggle for Ukraine*, p. 18

11 Richard Overy, *Russia's War* (1999 e-book edition)

12 Carroll, Oliver, Welcome to the Cossack People's Republic of Stakhanov, *Politico* website, 2 November 2014, https://www.politico.com/magazine/story/2014/11/welcome-to-the-cossack-peoples-republic-of-stakhanov-112420/

13 Abibok, 'On the way to creating the 'Donbas people' – Identity policy in the self-proclaimed republics in east Ukraine', p. 2

14 Abibok, 'On the way to creating the 'Donbas people' – Identity policy in the self-proclaimed republics in east Ukraine', p. 3

15 Puri, *Russia's Road to War with Ukraine*, p. 76

16 Mustafa Nayem, Uprising in Ukraine: How It All Began, *Open Society Foundations* website, 4 April 2014, https://www.opensocietyfoundations.org/voices/uprising-ukraine-how-it-all-began

17 Roman Goncharenko, Sharp escalation, *DW* website, 19 February 2014, https://www.dw.com/en/titushki-the-ukrainian-presidents-hired-strongmen/a-17443078

18 Arutunyan, *Hybrid Warriors: Proxies, Freelancers and Moscow's Struggle for Ukraine*, p. 47

19 Matveeva, Anna, *Through Times of Trouble – Conflict in southeastern Ukraine explained from within* (Lexington Books 2017 edition), pp. 63–64

20 Arutunyan, *Hybrid Warriors: Proxies, Freelancers and Moscow's Struggle for Ukraine*, p. 67

21 Malyarenko and Galbreath, 'Paramilitary motivation in Ukraine', p. 128

Chapter 2

1 Matveeva, *Through Times of Trouble – Conflict in Southeastern Ukraine Explained from Within*, pp. 98–99

2 Matveeva, *Through Times of Trouble – Conflict in Southeastern Ukraine Explained from Within*, p. 217

3 Matveeva, *Through Times of Trouble – Conflict in Southeastern Ukraine Explained from Within*, p. 99

4 Matveeva, *Through Times of Trouble – Conflict in Southeastern Ukraine Explained from Within*, p. 79

5 Now the city of Krivy-Rih in Ukraine. To this day the location of vast deposits of iron ore, it was the linking of the cities of Donetsk and Krivy-Rih by railway in the late nineteenth century that helped create the vast metal-working industrial enterprises of Donbas.

6 Vladimir Kornilov, «Донецко-Криворожская республика. Расстрелянная мечта» (2017), ISBN 978-5-496-03067-0.

7 Andrew Monaghan, *Russian Grand Strategy in the era of global power competition* (Manchester: Manchester University Press, 2022), p. xix

8 Charles Clover, *Black Wind, White Snow – The rise of Russia's new nationalism* (New Haven: Yale, 2016), p. 12

9 Puri, *Russia's Road to War with Ukraine*, p. 25

10 Clover, *Black Wind, White Snow – The rise of Russia's new nationalism*, p. 2

11 Marlene Laruelle, 'The three colors of Novorossiya, or the Russian nationalist mythmaking of the Ukrainian crisis', *Post-Soviet Affairs* (2016), 32:1, DOI: 10.1080/1060586X.2015.1023004, pp. 55–74

12 Ivan D. Loshkariov and Andrey A. Sushentsov, 'Radicalization of Russians in Ukraine: from 'accidental' diaspora to rebel movement', *Southeast European and Black Sea Studies*, 16:1 (2016), pp. 71–90, DOI: 10.1080/14683857.2016.1149349, p. 79

13 Pål Kolstø, 'Symbol of the War — But Which One? The St George Ribbon in Russian Nation-Building', *The Slavonic and East European Review*, Vol. 94, No. 4 (October 2016), pp. 665–666, https://doi.org/10.5699/slaveasteurorev2.94.4.0660

14 Adam Swain (ed.), *Re-constructing the Post-Soviet Industrial Region: The Donbas in transition* (Cambridge: Cambridge University Press, 2007)

15 Anon, 'Peace in Ukraine (III): The Costs of War in Donbas', *International Crisis Group*, Report No. 261 (3 Sept 2020), https://www.crisisgroup.org/europe-central-asia/eastern-europe/ukraine/261-peace-ukraine-iii-costs-war-donbas

16 Quoted in Malyarenko and Galbreath, 'Paramilitary Motivation in Ukraine', p. 129

Chapter 3

1 Sergei Medvedev, *The Return of the Russian Leviathan* (Cambridge: Polity 2020), p. 202

2 Clover, *Black Wind, White Snow – The rise of Russia's new nationalism*, p. 13

3 Matveeva, *Through Times of Trouble – Conflict in Southeastern Ukraine Explained from Within*, p. 203

4 Kolstø, 'Symbol of the War — But Which One? The St George Ribbon in Russian Nation-Building'

5 Artem Shevchenko, *Slovyansk: The Beginning of the War* (Kharkiv: Folio, 2020), p. 45

6 Daisy Sindelar, 'What's Orange And Black And Bugging Ukraine?', *Radio Free Europe* website, 28 April 2014, https://www.rferl.org/a/ukraine-colorado-beetle-separatists/25365793.html

Chapter 4

1 Yaffa, *Between Two Fires – Truth, ambition and compromise in Putin's Russia*, p. 275

2 Wood, *Russia Without Putin: Money, Power and the Myths of the New Cold War*, p. 133

3 Igor Sutyagin and Justin Bronk, *Russia's New Ground Forces: Capabilities, Limitations and Implications for International Security* (Abingdon: Routledge, 2017), p. 105

4 Puri, *Russia's Road to War with Ukraine*, p. 194

Chapter 5

1 Alec Luhn, Military assaults against pro-Russian occupiers rumoured in eastern Ukraine, *The Guardian* website, 10 April 2014, https://www.theguardian.com/world/2014/apr/10/military-assaults-rumoured-eastern-ukraine-russian

2 Luhansk prosecutors launch probes into federalization support rallies, *Interfax Ukraine* website, 21 April 2014, https://en.interfax.com.ua/news/general/201534.html

3 Marko Djuric, Ukraine Unrest: Separatists Seize Buildings In Horlivka, *Reuters* website, 30 April 2014, https://www.huffpost.com/entry/ukraine-unrest-separatists-seize-buildings_n_5237530

4 Oksana Grytsenko, Luhansk separatists say their chief wounded in assassination attempt, *Kyiv Post*, 13 May 2014; https://archive.kyivpost.com/article/content/war-against-ukraine/luhansk-separatists-say-their-chief-bolotov-wounded-347628.html

5 Oksana Grytsenko, Luhansk separatist leader Bolotov free in Ukraine after suspicious 'shootout', *Kyiv Post*, 17 May 2014, https://archive.kyivpost.com/article/content/war-against-ukraine/luhansk-separatist-leader-bolotov-free-in-ukraine-after-suspicious-shootout-348247.html

6 Insurgents assault Ukrainian border guards in Luhansk Oblast; at least 15 wounded, 5 dead, *Kyiv Post* website, 2 June 2014, https://archive.kyivpost.com/ukraine-politics/insurgents-assault-ukrainian-border-guards-in-luhansk-oblast-350281.html

7 Diana Magnay and Tim Lister, Air attack on pro-Russian separatists in Luhansk kills 8, stuns residents, *CNN* website, 3 June 2014, https://edition.cnn.com/2014/06/03/world/europe/ukraine-luhansk-building-attack/index.html

8 Matveeva, *Through Times of Trouble – Conflict in southeastern Ukraine explained from within*, p. 162

9 Michael Kofman, Katya Migacheva, Brian Nichiporuk, Andrew Radin, Olesya Tkacheva and Jenny Oberholtzer, *Lessons from Russia's Operations in Crimea and Eastern Ukraine* (RAND Corporation, 2017), pp. 56–57

10 Lizzie Dearden, Ukraine crisis: Nato images show Russian soldiers, artillery and armoured vehicles in 'military operations' in eastern Ukraine, *The Independent* website, 29 August 2014, https://www.independent.co.uk/news/world/europe/ukraine-crisis-nato-images-show-russian-soldiers-artillery-and-armoured-vehicles-in-military-operations-in-eastern-ukraine-9698471.html

11 Ukraine crisis: Military plane shot down in Luhansk, *BBC News* website, 14 June 2014, https://www.bbc.co.uk/news/world-europe-27845313

12 Olha Stryzhova, Why the Battle for Luhansk Airport is just as important as the Battle for Donetsk Airport, *Euromaidan Press* website, 10 February 2018, https://euromaidanpress.com/2018/02/10/117926/

13 Stefan Huijboom, 'Quieter, but guns of war still not silent, on first day of cease-fire in Donetsk', *Kyiv Post*, 15 Feb 2015

14 Matveeva, *Through Times of Trouble – Conflict in southeastern Ukraine explained from within*, p. 136

15 Vladimir Socor, Armed Formations in the Secessionist 'Luhansk Republic' (Part Two), *Eurasia Daily Monitor,* Volume: 12 Issue: 9, 15 January 2015, https://jamestown.org/program/armed-formations-in-the-secessionist-luhansk-republic-part-two/

16 Обращение И Приказ Атамана Н. И. Козицына, 2014, http://vvd2003.narod.ru/

17 Казаки занимают Донбасс, 21 May 2014, https://web.archive.org/web/20170721053940/http://www.ng.ru/

18 Казаки занимают Донбасс, 21 May 2014, https://web.archive.org/web/20170721053940/http://www.ng.ru/

19 Vladimir Socor, Armed Formations in the Secessionist 'Luhansk Republic' (Part Two), *Eurasia Daily Monitor,* Volume: 12 Issue: 9, 15 January 2015, https://jamestown.org/program/armed-formations-in-the-secessionist-luhansk-republic-part-two/

20 Vladimir Socor, Armed Formations in the Secessionist 'Luhansk Republic' (Part Two), *Eurasia Daily Monitor,* Volume: 12 Issue: 9, 15 January 2015, https://jamestown.org/program/armed-formations-in-the-secessionist-luhansk-republic-part-two/

21 Justin Bristow, Russian Private Military Companies: An Evolving Set of Tools in Russian Military Strategy, FMSO, 26 August 2019, https://community.apan.org/wg/tradoc-g2/fmso/m/fmso-monographs/287870

22 Vladimir Socor, Armed Formations in the Secessionist 'Luhansk Republic' (Part Three), *Eurasia Daily Monitor,* Volume: 12 Issue: 10, 16 January 2015, https://jamestown.org/program/armed-formations-in-the-secessionist-luhansk-republic-part-three/

23 Matveeva, *Through Times of Trouble – Conflict in southeastern Ukraine explained from within,* p. 137

24 Vladimir Socor, Armed Formations in the Secessionist 'Luhansk Republic' (Part Three), *Eurasia Daily Monitor,* Volume: 12 Issue: 10, 16 January 2015, https://jamestown.org/program/armed-formations-in-the-secessionist-luhansk-republic-part-three/

25 Oleg Orlov, Ukraine's forgotten city destroyed by war, *The Guardian* website, 7 January 2015

26 Vladimir Socor, Armed Formations in the Secessionist 'Luhansk Republic' (Part Three), *Eurasia Daily Monitor,* Volume: 12 Issue: 10, 16 January 2015, https://jamestown.org/program/armed-formations-in-the-secessionist-luhansk-republic-part-three/

27 Один із ключових польових командирів невизнаної луганської республіки Павло Дрьомов загинув через підрив його автомобілю неподалік міста Ірміно. Також загинув його водій, *Hromadske Radio* website, 12 December 2015, http://hromadskeradio.org/2015/12/12/kazachyy-otaman-pavlo-dromov-zagynuv-vnaslidok-pidryvu-yogo-avtomobilyu

28 Donbass Coup D'état – an Analysis, *Warsaw Institute* website, 4 December 2017, https://warsawinstitute.org/donbass-coup-detat-analysis/

29 Stanytsia Luhanska Bridge is Broken, DFRLab, 2 November 2017, https://medium.com/dfrlab/stanytsia-luhanska-bridge-is-broken-97f577165db9

30 Sergiy Karazy, Bridge to peace? Zelenskiy unveils restored span in eastern Ukraine, *Reuters* website, 20 November 2019, https://www.reuters.com/article/uk-ukraine-crisis-bridge-idUKKBN1XU25Q

31 Donbass Coup D'état – an Analysis, *Warsaw Institute,* 4 December 2017, https://warsawinstitute.org/donbass-coup-detat-analysis/

32 У Луганську – конфлікт між Плотницьким і "головою МВС" Корнетом, *BBC Ukraine* website, 21 November 2017, http://www.bbc.com/ukrainian/news-42067886

33 Yuri Zoria, 'Coup attempt underway in occupied Luhansk: what we know so far', *Euromaidan Press* website, 22 November 2017, https://euromaidanpress.com/2017/11/22/coup-attempt-in-occupied-luhansk-what-we-know-so-far/

34 В "ДНР" и "ЛНР" объявлена всеобщая мобилизация, *DW* website, 19 Feb 2022, https://www.dw.com/ru/v-dnr-objavili-vseobshhuju-mobilizaciju/a-60839410

35 Глава ЛНР Пасечник подписал указ о всеобщей мобилизации в республике, *RT* website, 19 February 2022, https://russian.rt.com/ussr/news/964537-lnr-mobilizaciya-respublika

36 В ДНР и ЛНР военные силой забирают жителей на войну, URA Information Agency, 21 February 2022, https://ura.news/news/1052534219

37 Gleb Golod, 'Life here is going downhill' How forced mobilization has transformed the Donbas 'people's republics', *Meduza* website, 12 July 2022

38 Указ Президента Российской Федерации от 21.02.2022 № 71 "О признании Донецкой Народной Республики", http://publication.pravo.gov.ru/Document/View/0001202202220002

39 Обращение Президента Российской Федерации, 21 February 2022, http://kremlin.ru/events/president/news/67828

40 Путин: Россия признала ДНР и ЛНР в границах Донецкой и Луганской областей, *BBC News* website, 22 February 2022, https://www.bbc.com/russian/news-60483790

41 Росія почала військову окупацію частини Донбасу: з'явилось відео входження колони техніки, *TSN* website, 21 February 2022, https://tsn.ua/ato/rosiya-pochala-viyskovu-okupaciyu-chastini-donbasu-znyato-vhodzhennya-koloni-tehniki-1983349.html

42 В ЛНР заявили, что у республики не будет легкой операции в Донбассе, *Ria Novosti* website, 24 February 2022, https://ria.ru/20220224/lnr-1774683396.html?in=t

43 Оккупанты "ЛНР" объявили о начале штурма прифронтового Счастья (видео), *Focus* website, 24 February 2022, https://focus.ua/voennye-novosti/507625-okkupanty-lnr-obyavili-o-nachale-shturma-prifrontovogo-schastya-video

44 «Счастье не дадим потерять стране». Как жители города в Луганской области выживают во время обострения на фронте, *Hromadske* website, 24 February 2022, https://hromadske.ua/ru/posts/schaste-ne-dadim-poteryat-strane-kak-zhiteli-goroda-v-luganskoj-oblasti-vyzhivayut-vo-vremya-obostreniya-na-fronte

45 ВСУ отбили атаку на прифронтовое Счастье, город остается под контролем Украины, *Focus* website, 24 Fenruary 2022, https://focus.ua/voennye-novosti/507638-vsu-otbili-ataku-na-prifrontovoe-schaste-gorod-ostaetsya-pod-kontrolem-ukrainy

46 Плацдарменное положение: Луганская республика начала решающие бои, *Izvestia* website, 28 February 2022, https://iz.ru/1297865/anton-lavrov-platcdarmennoe-polozhenie-luganskaia-respublika-nachala-reshaiushchie-boi

47 The Joint Centre for Control and Coordination (JCCC, or СЦКК in both Russian and Ukrainian) was an organisation comprising both Ukrainian and Russian Federation military officers which was set up in 2014. The organisation's purpose was to monitor the Minsk ceasefire agreement. Eventually in December 2017 Russia withdrew its officers from the JCCC completely, effectively ceasing this form of cooperation. However, as cross-contact line 'cooperation' was still required, a few DPR and LPR armed formation officers were informally badged as 'JCCC' to continue some of the functions previously performed by the Russian officers. These armed formation JCCC officers had no de-jure recognition in this role by Ukraine.

48 В Станице Луганской российские оккупанты сняли украинские государственные символы со здания ВГА, *Depo*

Donbass website, 26 February 2022, https://dn.depo.ua/rus/severodonetsk/u-stanitsi-luganskiy-rosiyski-okupanti-znyali-ukrainski-derzhavni-simvoli-z-budivli-vtsa-202202261429127

49 Держзрада керівників селищної військово-цивільної адміністрації на Луганщині – розпочато розслідування, *Ukrainian Prosecutor's Office* website, 2 March 2022, https://www.gp.gov.ua/ua/posts/derzzrada-kerivnikiv-selishhnoyi-viiskovo-civilnoyi-administraciyi-na-luganshhini-rozpocato-rozsliduvannya

50 AFU destroyed 2 enemy tanks and 1 IFV near Triokhizbenka, Ukrainian Military TV YouTube channel, 25 February 2022, https://youtu.be/QA3s2-ViSNo

51 Город Счастье и семь поселков освобождены в ЛНР, *Don24* website, 28 February 2022, https://don24.ru/rubric/obschestvo/gorod-schaste-i-sem-poselkov-osvobozhdeny-v-lnr.html

52 "РАЗУМ ТВ" – 28.02.22 Освобождение Счастья, YouTube, 28 February 2022, https://youtu.be/mO0Uo8pfgPE

53 Захваченные Счастье и Станица Луганская почти уничтожены, люди в подвалах без воды и еды, *Liga News* website, 27 February 2022, https://news.liga.net/politics/photo/zahvachennye-schaste-i-stanitsa-luganskaya-pochti-unichtojeny-lyudi-v-podvalah-bez-vody-i-edy

54 Кольцевая линия: войска республик Донбасса и России блокировали Мариуполь, *Izvestia* website, 2 March 2022, https://iz.ru/1299052/roman-kretcul-bogdan-stepovoi-anton-lavrov-andrei-fedorov/vyzhat-vse-sroki-voiska-donbassa-i-rossii-soedinilis-pod-mariupolem

55 «Теперь работаем вместе». Войска ЛНР и армия России вышли навстречу друг другу в Донбассе, YouTube, 4 March 2022, https://youtu.be/m4JS55TTO_0

56 Луганское Счастье: как в ЛНР налаживают жизнь под залпы артиллерии, *Izvestia* website, 5 March 2022, https://iz.ru/1300846/anton-lavrov/luganskoe-schaste-kak-v-lnr-nalazhivaiut-zhizn-pod-zalpy-artillerii

57 Глава ЛНР заявил об освобождении от украинских военных порядка 80% территории республики; *TASS* website; 22 March 2022; https://tass.ru/mezhdunarodnaya-panorama/14142001

58 Глава ЛНР заявил об освобождении от украинских военных порядка 80% территории республики; *TASS* website; 22 March 2022; https://tass.ru/mezhdunarodnaya-panorama/14142001

59 Arutunyan, *Hybrid Warriors: Proxies, Freelancers and Moscow's Struggle for Ukraine*, p. 252

60 Gleb Golod, 'Life here is going downhill' How forced mobilization has transformed the Donbas 'people's republics', *Meduza* website, 12 July 2022

61 Gleb Golod, 'Life here is going downhill' How forced mobilization has transformed the Donbas 'people's republics', *Meduza* website, 12 July 2022

62 Mari Saito, Maria Tsvetkova and Anton Zverev, Abandoned Russian base holds secrets of retreat in Ukraine, *Reuters* website, 26 October 2022, https://www.reuters.com/investigates/special-report/ukraine-crisis-russia-base/

63 Russian invaders take control of Kreminna in Luhansk region – Haidai, *Ukrinform* website, 18 April 2022, https://www.ukrinform.net/rubric-ato/3460421-russian-invaders-take-control-of-kreminna-in-luhansk-region-haidai.html

64 Kateryna Tishenko, На Луганщині ЗСУ ліквідували відомого ватажка "ЛНР", *Ukrainska Pravda* website, 19 April 2022, https://www.pravda.com.ua/news/2022/04/19/7340742/

65 Martin Belam, Russia releases photo of cosmonauts holding Luhansk flag on ISS, *The Guardian* website, 4 July 2022, https://

www.theguardian.com/world/2022/jul/04/russian-cosmonauts-display-flag-of-occupied-luhansk-region-on-iss-ukraine

66 Sam Jones, Putin declares victory in Luhansk after fall of Lysychansk, *The Guardian* website, 4 July 2022, https://www.theguardian.com/world/2022/jul/04/ukraine-donetsk-next-russian-target-after-capture-of-luhansk-says-governor

67 Pavel Polityuk, Russia holds annexation votes; Ukraine says residents coerced, *Reuters* website, 24 September 2022, https://www.reuters.com/world/europe/ukraine-marches-farther-into-liberated-lands-separatist-calls-urgent-referendum-2022-09-19/

Chapter 6

1 Anon, 'How Russia controls occupied Donbas', *Ukrinform* website, 1 February 2021, https://www.ukrinform.net/rubric-polytics/3182285-how-russia-controls-occupied-donbas.html

2 Sutyagin and Bronk, Russia's New Ground Forces: Capabilities, Limitations and Implications for International Security, p. 111

3 Anon, 'Joint Forces Commander: Over 2,000 Russian career officers stationed in occupied Donbas', *Ukraine Ministry of Defence* website, 30 April 2020, https://www.mil.gov.ua/en/news/2020/04/30/joint-forces-commander-over-2-000-russian-career-officers-stationed-in-occupied-donbas/

4 As an example: Andrzej Wilk, 'Eyes west! A shift in focus in Russia's Southern Military District', *Centre for Eastern Studies* website, 8 September 2020, https://www.osw.waw.pl/en/publikacje/osw-commentary/2020-09-08/eyes-west-a-shift-focus-russias-southern-military-district

5 Anon, 'Direct dialogue with "L/DPR", COVID-19 and more – Weekly Update on Ukraine #10, 09 – 15 March', *Ukraine Crisis Media Centre* website, 16 March 2020, https://uacrisis.org/en/75240-weekly-update-ukraine-10-09-15-march

6 Freedman, *Ukraine and the Art of Strategy*, pp. 158–159

7 Matveeva, *Through Times of Trouble – Conflict in southeastern Ukraine explained from within*, p. 184

8 Anon, 'Intelligence data on 1st and 2nd Army Corps of Russian Federation in occupied Donbas', *InformNapalm* website, 8 September 2020, https://informnapalm.org/en/intelligence-data-on-1st-and-2nd-army-corps-of-russian-federation-in-occupied-donbas/

9 Arutunyan, *Hybrid Warriors: Proxies, Freelancers and Moscow's Struggle for Ukraine*, p. 10

Chapter 7

1 «Армейские корпуса» реорганизовали в «оперативно-тактические объединения», обновлён командный состав – данные исследования «СтопТеррор», *Ukraine Crisis Media Centre* website, 11 August 2016, https://uacrisis.org/ru/45994-kabakaev

2 1-Й И 2-Й АРМЕЙСКИЕ КОРПУСА, КАК УДАРНЫЕ ОБЪЕДИНЕНИЯ СУХОПУТНЫХ ВОЙСК РОССИИ НА ДОНБАССЕ, *OPK* website, 31 May 2023, https://opk.com.ua

3 Anon, '70% бойовиків на Донбасі – громадяни Росії, 25% – кадрові військові та 45% – так звані «добровольці», – воєнна розвідка', *Ukraine Crisis Media Centre* website, 17 April 2016, https://uacrisis.org/uk/42505-voyenna-rozvidka-2

4 Anon, 'Intelligence data on 1st and 2nd Army Corps of Russian Federation in occupied Donbas', *InformNapalm* website, 8 September 2020, https://informnapalm.org/en/intelligence-data-on-1st-and-2nd-army-corps-of-russian-federation-in-occupied-donbas/

5 1-Й И 2-Й АРМЕЙСКИЕ КОРПУСА, КАК УДАРНЫЕ ОБЪЕДИНЕНИЯ СУХОПУТНЫХ ВОЙСК РОССИИ НА ДОНБАССЕ, *OPK* website, 31 May 2023, https://opk.com.ua

6   «ЛНР» ВМЕСТО АЭРОПОРТА ОТКРЫЛА ПАРК
    С ОРУЖИЕМ, КОТОРОЕ НАРУШАЕТ МИНСКИЕ
    СОГЛАШЕНИЯ, *Novosti Donbassa* website, 7 October 2019,
    https://novosti.dn.ua/ru/news/295731-lnr-vmesto-aehroporta-
    otkryla-park-soruzhyem-kotoroe-narushaet-mynskye-
    soglashenyya

7   Anon, 'Intelligence data on 1st and 2nd Army Corps of Russian
    Federation in occupied Donbas', *InformNapalm* website, 8
    September 2020, https://informnapalm.org/en/intelligence-
    data-on-1st-and-2nd-army-corps-of-russian-federation-in-
    occupied-donbas/

8   2-я ОТДЕЛЬНАЯ МОТОСТРЕЛКОВАЯ БРИГАДА 2-го АК
    НМ ЛНР "сборник фотофактов", *LiveJournal* website, 29 April
    2015, https://ce48.livejournal.com/4135.html

9   Matveeva, *Through Times of Trouble – Conflict in southeastern
    Ukraine explained from within*, p. 135

10 Бригада имени Ворошилова, colonelcassad LiveJournal
    page, 5 September 2016, https://colonelcassad.livejournal.
    com/2940275.html

11 Комбат батальона спецназначения ЛНР «Леший» о службе и
    войне, *Russkaya Vesna* website, 11 October 2014, https://rusvesna.
    su/news/1413015517

12 Секрет Бэтмена, Ura.ru website, 17 December 2014, https://ura.
    news/articles/1036263680

13 Бедный Бэтмен, Ura.ru website, 3 January 2015, https://ura.news/
    articles/1036263795

14 Российская 15-я миротворческая бригада просто переоделась
    в террористов "ЛНР". Доказательство. ФОТОрепортаж,
    Censor.net website, 19 September 2014, https://censor.net/
    ru/p303340

15 The War Criminals of the 15th 'Peacekeeping' Brigade:
    Unpublished Story, *InformNapalm* website, 3 June 2016,
    https://informnapalm.org/en/mar06-war-criminals-15th-
    peacekeeping-brigade/

16 Matveeva, *Through Times of Trouble – Conflict in southeastern
    Ukraine explained from within*, p. 135

17 Vladimir Socor, Armed Formations in the Secessionist 'Luhansk
    Republic' (Part Four), *Eurasia Daily Monitor*, Volume: 12 Issue:
    10, 16 January 2015, https://jamestown.org/program/armed-
    formations-in-the-secessionist-luhansk-republic-part-four/

18 Matveeva, *Through Times of Trouble – Conflict in southeastern
    Ukraine explained from within*, p. 135

19 Силы ЛНР разбили бронеавтомобиль, подаренный
    Жириновским, KP.ua website, 15 September 2014, https://kp.ua/
    politics/470211-syly-lnr-razbyly-broneavtomobyl-podarennyi-
    zhyrynovskym

20 Matveeva, *Through Times of Trouble – Conflict in southeastern
    Ukraine explained from within*, p. 136

21 Командир луганской бригады «Призрак»: «Никто другой
    Стрелкова не заменит», MK.ru website, 28 August 2014, https://
    www.mk.ru/politics/2014/08/28/komandir-luganskoy-brigady-
    prizrak-nikto-drugoy-strelkova-ne-zamenit.html

22 Russia-Backed Separatists Conduct Explosive Training Exercises,
    DFRLab website, 14 April 2017, https://medium.com/dfrlab/
    russia-backed-separatists-conduct-explosive-training-exercises-
    111c63f77fe

23 Под Бахмутом погибли российский комбриг и замполит
    корпуса, *Radio Svoboda* website, 14 May 2023, https://www.
    svoboda.org/a/pod-bahmutom-pogibli-rossiyskiy-kombrig-i-
    zampolit-korpusa/32411064.html

24 Бригада двух республик, oneparatrooper LiveJournal page, 21
    June 2016, https://oneparatrooper.livejournal.com/15848.html

25 A Soviet or Russian *divizion* (Russian: дивизион) is a unit of
    artillery equivalent to a battalion, not to be confused with the
    much larger 'division' in English (Russian: дивизия)

26 Пасечник присвоил Чистяковской бригаде Народной
    милиции почетное звание Гвардейской, *Lug-info* website, 10
    October 2018, https://lug-info.com/news/pasechnik-prisvoil-
    chistyakovskoi-brigade-narodnoi-militsii-pochetnoe-zvanie-
    gvardeiskoi-foto-39100

27 10-я артиллерийская бригада ЛНР, Militarizm LiveJournal page,
    21 February 2016, https://militarizm.livejournal.com/100157.html

28 10-я артиллерийская бригада ЛНР, Militarizm LiveJournal page,
    21 February 2016, https://militarizm.livejournal.com/100157.html

29 10-я артиллерийская бригада ЛНР, Militarizm LiveJournal page,
    21 February 2016, https://militarizm.livejournal.com/100157.html

30 Russian Giatsint-B artillery and Ural-632301 detected by
    aerial recon in Donbas, *InformNapalm* website, 11 July 2016,
    https://informnapalm.org/en/russian-artillery-detected-aerial-
    recon-donbas/

31 ГТРК ЛНР. 9 мая ПАРАД ПОБЕДЫ 2017 перезалить,
    YouTube website, 22 February 2022, https://www.youtube.com/
    watch?v=vPUuemRrrdg

32 Russia-Backed Separatists Conduct Explosive Training Exercises,
    DFRLab website; 14 April 2017; https://medium.com/dfrlab/
    russia-backed-separatists-conduct-explosive-training-exercises-
    111c63f77fe

33 Russia-Backed Separatists Conduct Explosive Training Exercises,
    DFRLab website; 14 April 2017; https://medium.com/dfrlab/
    russia-backed-separatists-conduct-explosive-training-exercises-
    111c63f77fe

34 Комендантский полк ЛНР отметил вторую годовщину
    образования, *Lug-info* website, 21 November 2016, https://
    lug-info.com/news/komendantskii-polk-lnr-otmetil-vtoruyu-
    godovschinu-obrazovaniya-19172

35 4-й Отдельный Танковый Батальон 2-го АК НМ ЛНР,
    фотосборник, ce48 LiveJournal page, 7 July 2015, https://ce48.
    livejournal.com/4643.html

36 4-й Отдельный Танковый Батальон 2-го АК НМ ЛНР,
    фотосборник, ce48 LiveJournal page, 7 July 2015, https://ce48.
    livejournal.com/4643.html

37 Павшие герои Освободительного похода (БТО №12), yadocent
    LiveJournal page, 11 March 2022, https://yadocent.livejournal.
    com/1429693.html

38 1-Й И 2-Й АРМЕЙСКИЕ КОРПУСА, КАК УДАРНЫЕ
    ОБЪЕДИНЕНИЯ СУХОПУТНЫХ ВОЙСК РОССИИ НА
    ДОНБАССЕ, *OPK* website, 31 May 2023, https://opk.com.ua

39 1-Й И 2-Й АРМЕЙСКИЕ КОРПУСА, КАК УДАРНЫЕ
    ОБЪЕДИНЕНИЯ СУХОПУТНЫХ ВОЙСК РОССИИ НА
    ДОНБАССЕ, *OPK* website, 31 May 2023, https://opk.com.ua

40 'Life here is going downhill' How forced mobilization has
    transformed the Donbas 'people's republics', *Meduza* website, 12
    July 2022, https://meduza.io/en/feature/2022/07/12/life-here-is-
    going-downhill. The video mentioned in the article had by the
    time of writing been taken down.

41 ГумФронт. Сбор на 206 полк. с 28.09.22, YouTube website, 26
    September 2022, https://www.youtube.com/watch?v=9spNI-4xx7g

Chapter 8

1   ГТРК ЛНР. 9 мая ПАРАД ПОБЕДЫ 2021 Года перезалить,
    YouTube website, 18 February 2022, https://youtu.be/KHl5p4J1wzI

Chapter 9

1 На Луганщине боевики похитили две БРДМ из пожарно-спасательных частей, *Unian* website, 18 May 2014, https://www.unian.net/politics/919161-na-luganschine-boeviki-pohitili-dve-brdm-iz-pojarno-spasatelnyih-chastey.html

2 Verbatim Record in the case concerning Application of the International Convention for the Suppression of the Financing of Terrorism and of the International Convention on the Elimination of All Forms of Racial Discrimination (Ukraine v. Russian Federation), 7 March 2017, International Court of Justice The Hague, pp. 20–21

3 Российская 15-я миротворческая бригада просто переоделась в террористов "ЛНР". Доказательство. ФОТОрепортаж, Censor.net website, 19 September 2014, https://censor.net/ru/p303340

4 Vera Zimmerman, 'The Role of Snipers in the Donbas Trench War', *Eurasia Daily Monitor,* Volume 17 Issue 26, 25 Feb 2020, https://jamestown.org/program/the-role-of-snipers-in-the-donbas-trench-war/

5 Актуальные ПТРСы и ПТРДэшки, viktorshestakov LiveJournal page, 29 August 2015, https://viktorshestakov.livejournal.com/408661.html

6 На Луганщине в доме боевика нашли арсенал оружия, Ukrainskaya Pravda, 12 May 2018, https://www.pravda.com.ua/rus/news/2018/05/12/7180114/

7 Anon, 'Не можна виявити металошукачами: нові поставки мін росіянами на Донбас', *Militarny* website, 9 July 2018, https://mil.in.ua/uk/ne-mozhna-vyyavyty-metaloshukachamy-novi-postavky-min-rosiyanamy-na-donbas/

8 Т-64БМ "БУЛАТ", В ВОЙНЕ НА ДОНБАССЕ. ЧАСТЬ 3. Трофеи, andrewbek_1974 LiveJournal page, 7 February 2017, https://andrewbek-1974.livejournal.com/180264.html

9 Танки Т-72 Ополчения, mishaxaxa LiveJournal page, 13 January 2015, https://mishaxaxa.livejournal.com/419.html

10 Наблюдатели InformNapalm посетили базу хранения танков Т-64, Т-72 и Т-72С1 под Луганском, *InformNapalm* website, 18 February 2016, https://informnapalm.org/20024-tanki/

11 Переброшенные на Донбасс танки Т-62М с усиленной защитой появились на фронте, Topwar.ru website, 18 June 2022, https://topwar.ru/197945-perebroshennye-na-donbass-tanki-t-62m-s-usilennoj-zaschitoj-pojavilis-na-fronte.html

12 Башни от БМП-1 установили на МТ-ЛБ в ЛНР, RG.ru website, 24 March 2022, https://rg.ru/2022/03/24/bashni-ot-bmp-1-ustanovili-na-mt-lb-v-lnr.html

13 Anon, 'OSCE spots 15 newest Russian UAZ Esaul armored vehicles in Donbas (Drone photo)', *InformNapalm* website, 3 May 2021, https://informnapalm.org/en/osce-spots-15-newest-russian-uaz-esaul-armored-vehicles-in-donbas-drone-photo/

14 ГТРК ЛНР. 9 мая ПАРАД ПОБЕДЫ 2021 Года перезалить, YouTube website, 18 February 2022, https://www.youtube.com/watch?v=KHl5p4J1wzI. The UAZ vehicles can be seen around the 42:35 timestamp.

15 Sutyagin and Bronk, *Russia's New Ground Forces: Capabilities, Limitations and Implications for International Security*, p. 58

16 Mikhailo Zhirokhov, САУ 2С3 «Акация» ЗСУ в ході війни на Донбасі (2014–2015), *Ukrainian Military Page*s website, 6 January 2016, https://www.ukrmilitary.com/2016/01/2s3-akacija.html

17 Бойцы ЛНР создали новую модификацию самоходки "Нона-С", RG.ru website, 23 March 2022, https://rg.ru/2022/03/23/bojcy-lnr-sozdali-novuiu-modifikaciiu-samohodki-nona-s.html

18 Alec Luhn, 'Bloodiest day in Ukraine conflict as rebel missiles bring down military jet', *The Guardian* website, 14 June 2014, https://www.theguardian.com/world/2014/jun/14/ukraine-conflict-bloodiest-day-missiles-bring-down-military-jet

19 Anon, 'Russian radars detected in eastern Ukraine', *DFR Lab* website, 11 March 2021, https://medium.com/dfrlab/russian-radars-detected-in-eastern-ukraine-fb625ec4de16

20 The criminal investigation by the Joint Investigation Team (JIT), *Netherlands Prosecution Service* website, undated, https://www.prosecutionservice.nl/topics/mh17-plane-crash/criminal-investigation-jit-mh17

21 Simon Shuster, 'How Russia Is Blocking Justice for the Victims of Flight 17', *Time Magazine* website, 17 July 2015, https://time.com/3963346/mh17-malaysia-airlines-flight-17-russia-ukraine/

22 Return to the MH17 Crash Site: Russian Roulette (Dispatch 87), YouTube website, 19 November 2014, https://youtu.be/cYEH6Tfzouo

23 Тарасовка – Облет позиций, YouTube website, 7 October 2014, https://youtu.be/k_oXGSWW_M8

24 Separatists Parade Military Equipment in Donetsk and Luhansk, *DFRLab* website, 11 May 2017, https://medium.com/dfrlab/separatists-parade-military-equipment-in-donetsk-and-luhansk-a067bf2f315c

25 Су-25 ополчения ЛНР, YouTube website, 29 January 2015, https://www.youtube.com/watch?v=qDMYUbQUVuo

26 Anon, 'Росія на Донбасі використовує більше 8 типів БПЛА', *InformNapalm* website, 22 March 2019, https://informnapalm.org/ua/rosiia-na-donbasi-vykorystovuie-bilshe-8/

27 Advanced Russian artillery reconnaissance system Navodchik-2 spotted in Donbas for the first time, *InformNapalm* website, 20 November 2020, https://informnapalm.org/en/advanced-russian-ew-system-navodchik-2-spotted-in-donbas-for-the-first-time/

28 Начальник розвідки 2 АК ЗС РФ під контролем UCA. Part 1: БЛА «Орлан-10»; *InformNapalm* website, 5 January 2017, https://informnapalm.org/ua/2-ak-zs-rf-pid-kontrolem-uca-part-1/

29 Anon, 'Российские системы РЭБ на Донбассе стали чаще попадать на фото. Эксклюзивные данные', *InformNapalm* website, 13 March 2020, https://informnapalm.org/48525-rossijskie-sistemy-reb-na-donbasse/

30 Михаил Жирохов, Украинский арсенал: плавающий транспортер ПТС-2, 11 December 2020, https://fraza.com/analytics/296321-ukrainskij-arsenal-plavajuschij-transporter-pts-2-

31 Михаил Жирохов, Украинский арсенал: плавающий транспортер ПТС-2, 11 December 2020, https://fraza.com/analytics/296321-ukrainskij-arsenal-plavajuschij-transporter-pts-2-

32 Единственный экземпляр: бронированную машину "Держатель" показали в ЛНР, RG.ru website, 12 May 2021, https://rg.ru/2021/05/12/edinstvennyj-ekzempliar-bronirovannuiu-mashinu-derzhatel-pokazali-v-lnr.html

Chapter 10

1 Russia spends about US$2 bln per year on "LPR/DPR" – Putin's ex-advisor, *Unian* website, 19 November 2018, https://www.unian.info/politics/10342539-russia-spends-about-us-2-bln-per-year-on-lpr-dpr-putin-s-ex-advisor.html